The Project Approach
in Early Years Provision

A practical guide to promoting children's creativity and critical thinking through project work

by Marianne Sargent

3-7 YEARS

Contents

About this book	**2**	Identifying an interest	41
		Open-ended planning	45
An introduction to the project approach	**3**	The role of the practitioner	51
What the project approach involves	3	Concluding the project	65
The project approach in early years provision	6	**Part Three: Communicating the approach**	**69**
Part One: Supporting early learning	**9**	Explaining the rationale behind the approach	69
A child-centred approach to teaching and learning	9	Demonstrating how the approach works in practice	69
Developmentally appropriate practice	22	**Further information**	**72**
Learning together	31	**References**	**73**
Part Two: The project approach in action	**41**	**Index**	**78**
A cyclical process	41	**Acknowledgements**	**80**

Published by Practical Pre-School Books, A Division of MA Education Ltd, St Jude's Church, Dulwich Road, Herne Hill, London, SE24 0PB.

Tel: 020 7738 5454

www.practicalpreschoolbooks.com

© MA Education Ltd 2011

All photos © MA Education Ltd. Photos taken by Ben Suri and Marianne Sargent.

Front cover photo: © iStockphoto.com/Sergey Galushko.
Photo on page 12 of the Learning Story on the CD-Rom © iStockphoto.com/Danielle Davey

ISBN 978-1-907241-17-8

About this book

This book is intended for early years leaders, trainers, practitioners and students. It aims to provide a guide to the project approach that links theory and research to practice and explains the approach using case study examples to bring it to life.

The book is divided into three parts. The first part entitled 'Supporting Early Learning' begins with an explanation of what the project approach is. It provides a rationale for using the approach by demonstrating how it fosters particular aspects of educational practice that support early learning. In doing so, it refers to learning theory and research and includes a number of case studies in order to illustrate how project work is beneficial to early educational practice. It also considers the general aims and principles of British early years curricula and how the project approach relates to these and helps to meet requirements. Additionally, it looks at issues and concerns surrounding using such an approach within early years settings.

The second part, called 'The Project Approach in Action' explains how project work is planned and carried out and provides examples of planning, observation and assessment documents. It explains how a full-scale project can be planned to lead on from a provocation, and provides a detailed description and photographs of a project carried out in a maintained inner-city community school nursery. Throughout, there are links to a number of adaptable and printable planning and observation documents, which are contained on a separate CD-Rom attached to the inside front cover of this book.

At the end of the book there is a guide for early years leaders as well as trainers and further education providers. It contains advice on how to communicate the approach to others and ideas for training exercises. This guide is supported with resources on the CD-Rom, including PowerPoint presentations for use as training aids.

The term practitioner is used throughout this book to refer to any professional working with young children in the early years sector.

The book provides case study examples throughout

This book explains how to plan, document and assess project work

An introduction to the project approach

Current thinking supports practice that involves promoting independence in young children and giving them the tools to become proficient learners as they continue through their education (DCELLS, 2008a; DCSF, 2008; Featherstone and Featherstone, 2008; Glazzard et al, 2010). In recent years policy makers and researchers have placed emphasis on the importance of enabling children to take control of their learning. The integration of Assessment for Learning methods into the Primary Strategies, as well as the focus upon critical thinking skills and the promotion of sustained shared thinking in the Early Years Foundation Stage (EYFS) guidance for England are other examples of this shift.

The project approach is a child-centred teaching strategy that enables children to follow their interests and fascinations, while developing the independence, knowledge and thinking skills they will need to become life-long learners.

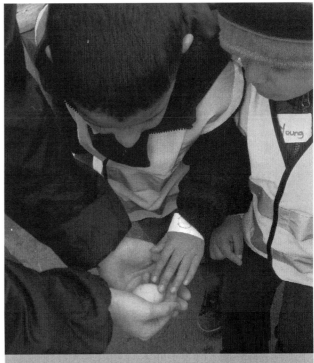

During a farm visit some nursery children were particularly interested in chicken eggs, which triggered a project all about eggs

What the project approach involves

Early years practitioners will be familiar with the use of themes and topics when planning curriculum delivery. It is common practice to choose a new topic each half term and plan subject related activities around it. For example, practitioners might use a topic about growing as inspiration for planning activities across all six areas of learning. For example, mathematical activities might include measuring the heights of children or bean stalks; literacy skills might be practised in a role-play gardening centre as children take on different roles; physical activities may involve playing jumping bean games; children may develop knowledge and understanding by growing their own bean plants; they might create collages with paper petals; and they could share pictures of themselves as babies and find out about the needs of young children.

Such activities serve their purpose and teach a range of knowledge and skills. However, although the overarching theme helps to create some commonality between areas of learning, teaching in this way can be disjointed and children often only scratch the surface in terms of learning any in-depth knowledge about the focus topic.

The project approach entails taking an area of interest – which may stem from a topic – and using this as a basis for in-depth enquiry or research. Areas of learning are not simply linked by a topic or theme; they are integrated as a result of the investigative process. Knowledge and skills are not taught in isolation, but rather acquired and practised within a meaningful context that makes sense to children. All projects stem from the interests of the children

Projects give children practical opportunities
to develop their knowledge and understanding
of how the world works

and are planned or developed in collaboration with
children. This is in contrast to topics that might have
initially been suggested by the children, but are
ultimately "adult-controlled" (Nutbrown, 2006, p.33).

Carrying out a project

An idea for a project will usually come from
practitioners' observations of the children in their
care. Such observations might highlight a particular
interest that has the potential to be developed into a
large-scale investigation or project.

A project is started with an initial provocation, such
as an event, question, picture or object that triggers
conversation and debate. After the children have
had some time to explore the provocation, they
are gathered together to share their experiences
and think about what they would like to find out
or do next. The children's questions, ideas and
suggestions are recorded and practitioners meet
together to discuss and use these as the basis
for planning the project. Practitioners then set up
various resources around the setting that will help
facilitate the children's explorations. The children

might investigate individually, in groups or as a
class and practitioners work alongside them to help
develop and extend ideas. This means observing
the children while they are working and perceptively
helping them to share and sustain thinking with
carefully considered open questioning.

Observation is a fundamentally important part of
project work and practitioners plan to ensure that
children's investigations are thoroughly documented
using written and photographic observations, as
well as digital recordings. Any work the children
produce is also kept or photographed. These
observations are used formatively to help plan the
direction of the ongoing project. At the conclusion
of the project, the documentation is used as a tool
for reflection and shared with the children. This
might be in the form of a learning story, where the
children look back at what they did and hear their
conversations and comments read back to them.

The project approach to teaching and learning
is not new. Froebel recognised that all areas of
knowledge were interrelated and that children
should be taught "to know the inner relations of
things to one another" (1887, quoted in Bruce,
2005, p.17). Isaacs' substantial records of her
observations at the Malting House School describe
a range of investigations from children weighing
each other using a see-saw, to digging up a dead
rabbit to find out if "it's gone up to the sky" (1930,
p.41). Isaacs' observations led her to realise that
if children are provided with opportunities to
investigate their fascinations they will develop
skills in applying knowledge to inform reasoning.
In addition, the Plowden Report advocated an
integrated curriculum because "rigid division of
the curriculum into subjects tends to interrupt
children's trains of thought and interest and to
hinder them from realising the common elements
in problem solving" (CACE, 1967, p.197). The
report recommended project work because it
"cuts across the boundaries of subjects" (CACE,
1967, p.199). Current British early years curricula
also support an integrated approach to curriculum
delivery (CCEA, 2006; DCELLS, 2008a; The Scottish
Government, 2008): "Although [the areas of learning
and development] are presented as six areas, it is
important to remember that for children everything
links and nothing is compartmentalised." (DCSF,
2007, Principles into Practice Card 4.4).

Lilian Katz and Sylvia Chard

The project approach in a contemporary context

In *Engaging Children's Minds* Katz and Chard (2000) describe a project as follows:

We use the term project to refer to an in-depth study of a particular topic... a project is a piece of research about a topic – one that may be related to a larger theme – in which children's ideas, questions, theories, predictions, and interests are major determinants of the experiences provided and the work accomplished.
(Katz and Chard, 2000, pp.2 and 5).

According to their model a project is divided into three phases:

■ the first phase is the planning stage whereby the practitioner finds out what the children already know about the subject and what they would like to find out;

■ the second phase is the actual investigation, involving research and field work;

■ the final phase entails drawing the project to a close with an event or display of the children's work.

Key thinking on project-based learning

Professor Lilian Katz and Professor Sylvia Chard are long-term project approach advocates and key thinkers in this area. Over the past 20 years they have extensively researched how the approach can be used with children to develop a range of skills and dispositions and further their learning.

The example project in the second part of this book is based upon the framework provided by Katz and Chard (1989; 2000) and Helm and Katz (2001). The structure this provides should prove a useful outline for practitioners to use as a starting point to plan their own projects.

Reggio Emilia, Northern Italy

The project approach in an international context

At the beginning of the school year practitioners in Reggio Emilia consult with children and together they decide upon possible long-term projects. A project is often introduced by showing the children something that triggers curiosity and discussion. This is known as a provocation and might be a piece of artwork, an object, a photograph or the documentation from a previous project, which acts as "a stimulus or thought provoker that invites wonder, curiosity and investigation" (Thornton and Brunton, 2007, p.69). The children are given time to digest the provocation, think about it and formulate questions and ideas. They then develop these thoughts into an idea for investigation and think of a title for the project.

A small-scale project might span just a couple of weeks and involve a class, group or individual. However, larger-scale projects can last as long as a couple of years and may involve a whole year group, school or the wider community. Throughout the life of a project, practitioners observe and compile a written and photographic record of the children's investigations. This is referred to as documentation and is considered an important teaching resource that is used to help the children reflect upon their learning.

Project work involves taking an interest and using it as a basis for in-depth enquiry or research

Project work is also central to the renowned Reggio Emilia Approach in Northern Italy, where in the absence of a formal curriculum, practitioners start with and build upon the curiosities of the children through the planning of *progettazione* or projects. Emphasis is placed upon group learning and discussion, with an aim to encourage children to engage in collaborative creative thinking with other children and adults to further their knowledge and understanding.

Documentation is centrally important to the Reggio Approach and is viewed as an extremely valuable resource for a number of reasons: for practitioners it serves as a useful formative assessment tool; for children it provides a means of facilitating reflective thought; and for parents it creates a picture of their children's learning (Thornton and Brunton, 2007). The explanation about planning, observation and assessment in the second part of this book is very much influenced by the Reggio Emilia approach to documentation.

Projects and provocations

Throughout the book references are made to both provocations and projects. They are defined as follows:

Provocation – The idea of a provocation has been adopted from Reggio Emilia where projects are triggered by initial thought-provokers or provocations. Anything can be used to provoke an investigation, including objects, pictures, events or questions.

Project – A project is planned to lead on from a provocation. Katz and Chard's (1989; 2000) model consists of three parts: practitioners and children first plan a project together; the children then carry out their investigations with the help and guidance of the practitioners; the project is drawn to a close with some form of presentation.

Projects can be planned with varying degrees of complexity. A practitioner may simply decide to set up a provocation, take a step back and observe while the children embark upon an open-ended investigation that has no set structure or format. The practitioner's role in this case is to observe the children and act as facilitator, providing the resources they need for their activities. The cocoon, frozen balloons and where is George provocations in the first part of the book are examples of this. On the other hand, a practitioner may decide to set

up a provocation with the intention of developing it into a full-scale planned project. The all about eggs project featured in the second part of the book is an example of this more complex and structured approach.

The project approach in early years provision

Many of the examples used throughout this book have been taken from foundation stage classrooms in maintained schools. However, the rich learning opportunities that project work presents are not restricted to these settings. The flexible nature of the approach makes it possible to adapt to any type of early years provision, including home-based provision. Projects can be undertaken in a one-to-one situation, with small groups, with a class, or even a whole school. The following three examples show how a variety of settings have used the project approach.

The first example demonstrates how a project can be carried out in a one-to-one situation within a restricted time-scale and with limited resources. The circumstances meant that the project needed a relatively tight structure and was adult-controlled to a large extent. However, it was still possible for the practitioner to choose an activity based upon the little boy's interests and share some control with him by enabling him to make his own informed choices about which materials to use when building his boat.

The project approach is just as applicable to practitioners who work in private settings with small numbers of mixed-age children. The size of the setting in the second example meant that there was less scope for providing an extensively wide variety of construction and craft materials that the children could experiment with and choose from. This was not practical for the childminder in terms of storage space or cost. However, the absence of a restrictive routine or timetable often associated with larger, maintained settings meant that she was able to devote a whole week to this project. The time available enabled her to fully involve the children throughout the whole project and children were able to design, plan and construct their own play mat. Furthermore, the scope of the project ensured that all of the children were involved regardless of age or

Teacher with one child

Snapshot example one

A teacher carried out this project with a five-year-old boy who was being schooled at home in Leeds while recovering from an illness. It took place during three two-hour sessions over a period of three weeks. The little boy was very interested in pirates and so the teacher decided to present him with a challenge to build a pirate ship that floats using his own choice of materials.

The teacher began with a floating and sinking exercise, inviting the child to try and float a variety of materials in a large tub of water. They tried paper, cardboard, plastic tubs, tinfoil, pieces of wood, corks, straws and plastic cutlery. They discussed what happened to each and talked about possible reasons why.

The teacher asked the boy to suggest which materials would be best for building his pirate ship and recorded his suggestions on a large sheet of paper. He then asked him what else he might need to build his boat and wrote these down too. He explained that he would gather all of the tools and materials needed by the following week.

With help from the teacher the little boy built his pirate ship using a margarine tub, with a straw for a mast, a paper sail and a skull and cross bones flag. They filled a bath with water and tested the ship, which remained afloat even with a toy pirate on board.

Childminder with a small group

Snapshot example two

This project was carried out with a group of four children aged between three and five in a private setting in Jersey over the period of one week. The practitioner had a tub of dinosaurs that the children very much enjoyed playing with. However, she did not have a play mat for the children to use in their imaginative play. She therefore decided to challenge the children to make a dinosaur land for this purpose.

She began by showing the children pictures from magazines and posters of how the Earth may have looked in prehistoric times. She also found some virtual CGI footage on the internet of dinosaurs roaming. She asked the children to point out and describe what they could see and recorded their comments. Using this list as a guide she helped the children to draw a plan of their play mat.

The practitioner collected a variety of junk materials and the following day she guided the children as they examined the sizes and shapes and chose various pieces to represent areas of landscape, i.e. yoghurt pots for volcanoes and large margarine tubs for hills. The children then stuck the various pieces onto a large thick piece of cardboard.

By the end of the week the children had covered the play landscape in mod-roc and painted it. They had sprinkled glitter into blue paint for rivers and lakes and stuck red and orange cellophane onto the sides of their volcanoes. They finished the project by coating the mat with watered down PVA glue to make it more durable.

ability. Each child contributed according to what their own skill set allowed, with older children sharing their knowledge and skills to help the younger ones.

Snapshot example three shows a larger-scale project carried out within a maintained school setting. The practitioner understood that the children needed time in order to get the most from the project and so

it was planned to run alongside the usual timetabled activities and routines over a period of several weeks. In addition, the practitioner knew that the arrival of the alien would cause a great deal of excitement initially and so planned for extra flexibility within the timetable during the first week. Furthermore, in the weeks that followed she ensured that any interesting learning opportunities that arose from the

Teacher and reception class

Snapshot example three

This provocation was set up in a reception class in a rural school in Newcastle and planned to fit into a topic about Space. Taking advantage of the woodland surroundings outside, the teacher put slime in the trees and set out a trail of clues that led the children to an alien hidden in some bushes. The alien was holding some photographs that had been taken the night before when he was exploring their classroom.

The alien explained his name was Zorg. He couldn't remember where he was from or what he was doing on Earth. The children decided he was from Mars and was lost. They decided he would be missing his family and so wanted to make him a spaceship to help him get back home. The teacher provided a large cardboard box and the children covered it in tinfoil and lined the inside with wallpaper. They cut up fabric to make a bed and drew pictures to stick on the walls. One little girl made a book for Zorg containing names and pictures of the children in the class.

This project lasted several weeks. During his stay Zorg was made very welcome by the children. He was taken to assemblies and ate lunch in the canteen. The children took turns to take him home and recorded their activities in a report book to share with everyone at school.

A couple of days after the spaceship was finished the children came into class to find it had disappeared and Zorg was gone. They found a thank you note explaining he had gone back to Mars to be with his family.

Then one morning the children came into class to find Zorg and the spaceship were gone. He left a note explaining he had gone back to Mars to be with his family.

provocation were developed as soon as practically possible by setting afternoons aside for this purpose. Issues concerning timetabling, curriculum coverage and other organisational dilemmas are especially pertinent for reception teachers and these are considered in more detail in relation to the cocoon provocation on page 10.

Projects can be carried out with children of any age. The aptitudes and abilities of the children will determine how complex a project becomes. Young children, or those with communication difficulties, will benefit from simple projects that encourage hands-on investigation and stimulate conversation, promoting language development. Older children, or those that have a broader knowledge base and better-developed academic skills, will be able to take part in more complex project work. The example used in the second part of this book demonstrates that as long as the subject matter is appropriate and there is sufficient adult support, it is possible to carry out a full-scale project with very young children who speak English as an additional language.

It is possible to carry out projects even with very young children

Part One: Supporting early learning

It is useful to look at the project approach in relation to early years practice that is recognised as conducive to effective early learning. In this section three provocations are featured and discussed, illustrating how various pedagogical aspects of project work support and promote children's learning. The discussion refers to the aims and principles of current British early years curricula and looks at how project work helps to meet requirements.

A child-centred approach to teaching and learning

The project approach is representative of a child-centred pedagogy that stems from a positive image of the young child as a competent learner who is capable of taking an active role in their education. The cocoon provocation featured in this section demonstrates the inclusive potential of projects and shows how they can enthuse children of all aptitudes and abilities, as well as motivate children to want to learn by building upon their interests. The discussion also considers the importance of giving children time, space and freedom to investigate phenomena in their own way and looks at the link between personal, social and emotional skills and cognitive development.

A positive image of the child

In Reggio Emilia, where projects are an integral part of early childhood education, the child is viewed as an "active constructor of knowledge" that is rich in potential (Hewett, 2001, p.96). Children are seen as apprentices for later life that have the ability to take an active role in their education:

We have a highly optimistic vision of the child: a child who possesses many resources at birth, and with an extraordinary potential which has never

Projects allow children to take control of their learning. Children are trusted to seek out information for themselves and empowered to find out more about what interests them

ceased to amaze us; a child with the independent means to build up its own thought processes, ideas, questioning and attempts at answers... (Malaguzzi, 2004, quoted in Bloomer and Cohen, 2008, p.16)

Rinaldi (2001) describes this as a democratic approach that supports the rights of children to actively participate in their education. Current British early years curricula documentation attempts to reflect a similar philosophy, promoting respect for children as individuals with a focus upon personal development and wellbeing, as well as academic achievement. The EYFS depicts a positive view of the child as a "competent learner" who is "resilient, capable and confident and self-assured" (DCSF, 2007, Principles into Practice Themes and Commitments Card). The Scottish Curriculum for

The Cocoon

Rawdon Littlemoor Primary School, Leeds

This provocation was set up in an Early Years Foundation Stage class of 45 reception children at a community primary school in Leeds. It was inspired by and planned to fit into a class topic on minibeasts. A fake cocoon constructed from a cereal box coated in paper-mâché and covered in green tissue paper was attached to the classroom ceiling with a toy minibeast inside.

All practitioners were instructed to ignore the cocoon until the children spotted it – which happened immediately on the first morning. Quite a stir was caused as they crowded around in a throng of interest. The classroom assistants and teachers observed their reactions, recording any questions, ideas and comments using clipboards and digital cameras. It was decided that the adults should not try to offer any suggestions or answers, but simply ask open questions, allowing the children to theorise and deliberate for themselves.

During the three weeks that followed, the cocoon was gradually opened to reveal the mystery minibeast. Its emergence caused a great deal of excitement, so much so, that on some occasions it was necessary to gather the children on the carpet and divide into talk partners. This encouraged them to engage in sustained discussion with one another and allowed them time to express their own views and consider the opinions of others.

Tom hatching from the cocoon

After the cocoon fully hatched the control of the project shifted over entirely to the children and the role of the adults became to help facilitate their ideas. The children named the creature Tom. They drew pictures of him and made food items and water bottles for him. They found out that Tom was related to Flik from the Pixar film *A Bug's Life*, and this led to an exchange of letters between the children and Flik over in America. Some children then began to bring in storybooks about Flik to share with the class.

Excellence states its purpose as "to enable each child or young person to be a successful learner, a confident individual, a responsible citizen and an effective contributor" (LTS, 2010). The Foundation Phase Framework for Children's Learning for 3 to 7-year-olds in Wales states an aim to ensure that children "are listened to" and "treated with respect" and maintains "children's own work should be respected, valued and encouraged for its originality and honesty" (DCELLS, 2008a, pp.3 and 5). Furthermore, the Northern Ireland Curriculum states its aim as to "empower young people to develop their potential" and views development as an individual as equally important to development as a citizen (CCEA, 2007, p.4).

There will always be curriculum documentation and policy guidance in place for early years educators to adhere to. There will also be an ever-increasing body of academic research that aims to help improve understanding of how young children learn and enhance foundation stage practice. Early years practitioners have the extremely difficult task of trying to deliver an age-appropriate curriculum, while under pressure to consider future Key Stage One requirements. It is therefore a case of balancing policy guidance, research findings, and knowledge founded on professional experience when deciding upon appropriate pedagogical approaches. It is also helpful for practitioners to consider how they view the children in their care. An appropriate teaching approach will trust and empower young children, motivating them to perform to the best of their abilities. The project approach entails breaking away – at least part of the time – from traditional curriculum delivery methods by enabling children to engage in imaginative and creative thought processes that lay the foundations for future independent learning. **When involved in project work children learn to think and find out for themselves instead of simply receiving information from others.**

Starting with the interests of the child

A basic principle underpinning the project approach is that projects should stem from the interests of the children (Katz and Chard, 2000). Nutbrown (2006) suggests that planning for learning that solely addresses curriculum requirements can limit the scope of possible learning outcomes, and narrow the opportunities for learning that might have occurred spontaneously if following the interests of children. Nutbrown proposes that practitioners should carefully observe young children's "threads of action

and thought" so as to gain a greater understanding of their interests and preoccupations (2006, p.34). Practitioners should then use these observations as a basis for planning teaching and learning that will interest and inspire the children. Any curriculum objectives covered can be highlighted after the fact. It is only possible to build on the interests of the children if practitioners spend time observing and documenting what they are interested in, as Dowling explains: "The possibilities for exploring the treasures of young children's minds are at their greatest if we note them when absorbed in their own ventures" (2008, p.14). Edwards describes this as "listening" to the children, explaining that observation and two-way discussion is "at the heart" of the Reggio Emilia teacher's role (1998, p.181).

There is a growing movement in Britain towards actively listening to young children and using their views and opinions to inform important decision-making processes (Gordon-Smith, 2011). The EYFS states that practitioners should "look at children's involvement" and give them control (DCSF, 2007, Principles into Practice Card 4.2) and the Welsh Foundation Phase Framework suggests that children are involved in planning discussions and mind mapping (DCELLS, 2008b). This means including children in planning processes and ensuring that plans are informed by knowledge of the children's individual interests and motivations (Young Children's Voices Network, 2010). **The project approach involves practitioners using their observations to identify predominant interests and schemas in children's activities before planning to develop these with related projects.**

The cocoon provocation shows how this works in practice. It was set up in response to the children's observed interest in butterflies. The children in this class had a fascination with the life cycle of the butterfly and the cocoon provocation was planned to build upon this. Caterpillars are not the only creatures that create cocoons and so the appearance of this one presented the children with a mystery that stirred their imaginations. The absence of a restrictive plan ensured that the practitioners were able to give the children time to consider and discuss their ideas about what might be inside. The children were then able to take control of events once the creature finally revealed itself. The practitioners continued to listen by

> ## Starting with the interests of the children: an example
>
> As part of a topic about minibeasts the children had read books including *The Case of the Missing Caterpillar* by Sam Godwin and *The Very Hungry Caterpillar* by Eric Carle. They had visited Tropical World, a visitor attraction housing various tropical plant and animal species, and seen a variety of real chrysalises and had first-hand observations of the class caterpillars' metamorphoses. This had been the cause of a great deal of discussion and interest. Many of the children had been observed drawing and painting pictures of caterpillars and butterflies.

The creature's appearance prompted
the children to draw his portrait

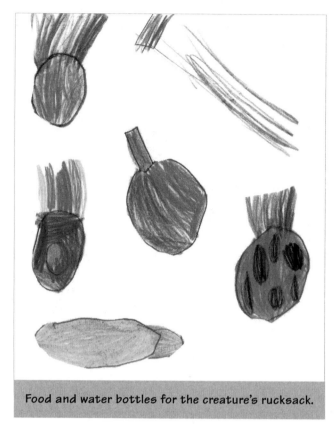

Food and water bottles for the creature's rucksack.

observing and allowed the provocation to unravel in line with the children's own thoughts and intentions. This allowed the children to engage in a range of spontaneous learning activities such as drawing pictures of the creature, showing him around the setting, including him in their play, making him food and water bottles for his rucksack and using construction materials to make him presents.

Project work involves actively listening to children through observation, then sharing, discussing and reflecting upon these observations with the children and other adults. The information gathered is then used to inform ongoing planning throughout the project. This process is explained in detail in part two of this book.

Time and space to think

Young children, like adults, need plenty of time to play around with ideas, discard some, improve others and allow them to take root. By doing this they start to make connections and so make genuine intellectual progress.
(Dowling, 2008, p.14)

Good quality early years provision comprises a varied and well-resourced learning environment that allows children freedom of choice, movement and space to engage in self-directed activity and exploration (DCSF, 2007). This is a view shared by early years pioneers including Montessori, Steiner and Froebel, as well as contemporary thinkers, such as Bruce, who advocates children being allowed to "wallow" in "free-flow play" and "first-hand experience" (Pound, 2008, p.13).

The Effective Early Learning project (Pascal and Bertram, 1997), which aimed to evaluate the quality of early years provision in Britain, drew upon the research of Professor Ferre Laevers. Laevers found that children need time to become absorbed in an activity without constant interruption if they are to become involved to a degree that significantly furthers their learning. Children operating at the highest level of involvement are "intrinsically motivated to continue and display signs of concentration, persistence, energy and complexity" (Pound, 2009, p.35). This can only occur if children are given sufficient time and space to become deeply involved and fully immersed in an activity. Csikszentmihayli (1998) describes this as being in flow. He suggests that if someone is given the opportunity to become fully engaged with

During a project children are given time and space to fully explore something that interests them

Time to explore and learn – missed opportunities: an example

"It's fake because cocoons don't have square patterns on." Jacob (age 4)

An opportunity was missed here to test Jacob's assertion. The class had some live chrysalises in a tank that could have been examined closely with magnifiers. Practitioners could also have helped Jacob find some pictures in information books and on the internet.

"I think it's just paper; the brown and white patchwork paper." James (age 4)

James was of course correct. The cocoon was constructed using cardboard covered in collaged tissue paper squares. In this case, it would have been a good idea to provide James with a variety of different types of craft paper and invite him to try and create the same effect to test his theory.

"Some air might be in there... might be loads and loads and it's cracked open." Lewis (age 5)

This was a great opportunity to explore the concept of force. There was a chance for Lewis to explain his idea and then test it with help; for example, paper bags could have been stuffed with sand until they burst and balloons pumped with air until they popped.

a task and allowed to channel all of her energy and concentration into it, then she will stretch herself and ultimately further her ability.

This is supported by the Key Elements of Effective Practice (KEEP) document, which highlights the importance of giving children "time to become engrossed" in their activities (DfES, 2005, p.11). Fragmented timetables with many activities can hinder a child's capacity to become engrossed in a topic and engage in deeper exploration. In contrast to this, project work involves children in extended periods of cross-curricular investigation and exploration. Children are allowed to concentrate on something that interests them. They are given time to explore every aspect of a particular area of interest and gather a large amount of in-depth information about it.

The cocoon provocation successfully grabbed the attention of the children and eventually led to them becoming involved in the free, self-directed activity and play, described on page 12. However, it was not until the final stage of the provocation that the children were given sufficient time and space to make this possible. When the cocoon first appeared the children were extremely excited and completely

absorbed in the mystery. At this point the children were gathered together to share their thoughts and the regular timetable was temporarily suspended for this purpose. However, once the initial excitement had died down, there was a return to timetable and the provocation was effectively paused until later in the day. A similar pattern prevailed throughout the duration of the provocation and whenever there was an interesting development the children were unable to fully explore their ideas. Each time chances were missed for the children to indulge in self-directed explorations, which could have potentially extended their learning. This might have been avoided if practitioners had suspended the timetable for the morning and allowed the children time to channel their energies into investigating the object that had captured their imagination so well. The children made some interesting statements in response to the provocation. If the curriculum had been more relaxed and the children's free time less structured, there would have been more scope for exploiting a number of learning opportunities, which were unfortunately missed. The learning opportunities described in the example on page 13 had further potential for offshoots of child-initiated investigation, which could have led in any number of directions had the children been given more time and space to become deeply involved in their own exploratory activities.

Practitioners are faced with a dilemma in terms of giving children time and independence while "retaining control over the curriculum" and maintaining routines (DCSF, 2007, Principles into Practice Card 4.2). Organisational dilemmas concerning timetabling and curriculum coverage

will differ across types of setting and the smaller more independent settings will have more freedom than larger maintained settings. It is up to individual practitioners to decide which approach will be best suited to their particular situation, although it may help to consider the following three aspects:

- Curriculum coverage

- The requirement to produce planning and evidence of learning

- Disruption to routines

Curriculum coverage

The holistic nature of the project approach means that opportunities are created for learning across all subject areas. Therefore, rather than regarding a project as an additional activity to be fitted in to an

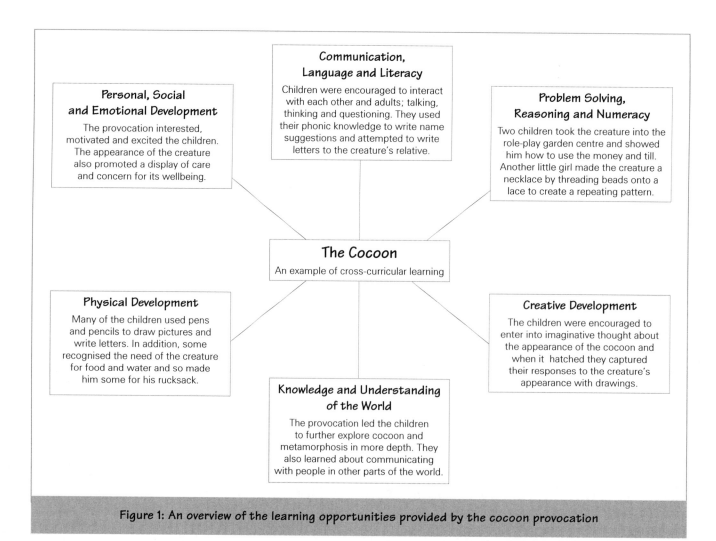

Personal, Social and Emotional Development
The provocation interested, motivated and excited the children. The appearance of the creature also promoted a display of care and concern for its wellbeing.

Communication, Language and Literacy
Children were encouraged to interact with each other and adults; talking, thinking and questioning. They used their phonic knowledge to write name suggestions and attempted to write letters to the creature's relative.

Problem Solving, Reasoning and Numeracy
Two children took the creature into the role-play garden centre and showed him how to use the money and till. Another little girl made the creature a necklace by threading beads onto a lace to create a repeating pattern.

The Cocoon
An example of cross-curricular learning

Physical Development
Many of the children used pens and pencils to draw pictures and write letters. In addition, some recognised the need of the creature for food and water and so made him some for his rucksack.

Creative Development
The children were encouraged to enter into imaginative thought about the appearance of the cocoon and when it hatched they captured their responses to the creature's appearance with drawings.

Knowledge and Understanding of the World
The provocation led the children to further explore cocoon and metamorphosis in more depth. They also learned about communicating with people in other parts of the world.

Figure 1: An overview of the learning opportunities provided by the cocoon provocation

already busy curriculum, it can be viewed as a useful vehicle for enabling cross-curricular delivery. Figure 1 shows that while involved in the cocoon provocation the children demonstrated learning in all six of the EYFS areas of learning and development.

If a provocation is allowed to develop naturally and the children are given sufficient time and space to explore and investigate there should be potential to cover a large number of curricula aims and goals:

> *When children are provided with simple, open-ended play materials in a sympathetic environment and their play and interaction is observed comprehensively, we would argue that the child-initiated activities can fulfil the adult-initiated objectives [of the EYFS]. (Broadhead and English, 2005, p.84).*

This is equally applicable to academic subjects, such as literacy and mathematics, and a detailed explanation of how projects can promote literacy in a developmentally appropriate way is provided on page 19. However, if there is something specific that a practitioner would like to cover, this can be planned to fit within the context of a project. For

Project work can be planned to fit around everyday routines

example, in this case, a practitioner hoping to do some work on pattern might specifically plan an activity that involves close inspection of the cocoon and comparing it with some real chrysalises, before asking the children to create some models of their own. Katz and Chard (2000) focus on the importance of providing time for spontaneous play, but acknowledge that children benefit from a variety of teaching methods, such as adult-led focused activities and direct instruction.

The requirement to produce planning and evidence of learning

The planning for a provocation needs to be open-ended, as it is the children's reactions that steer it any particular direction. This involves retrospective planning that initially identifies predicted outcomes but leaves space for recording actual learning outcomes as they occur during the provocation. This is retained as evidence of learning.

The planning for a full-scale project is slightly different. Control of the initial planning process is shared with the children, documented and kept on record. The project is then allowed to unfold without the constraint of pre-determined curriculum objectives, which ensures that spontaneous learning opportunities are followed up and capitalised on. Observations of the children's activities are later cross-referenced with curriculum documents and presented as evidence of learning. This process is explained in detail in the second part of this book.

O'Connor points out that the learning process can easily be "undervalued" in an educational climate that pushes practitioners to "focus on outcomes and competencies" (2008, pp.14-15). It might be suggested that the project approach supports practitioners by giving them license to allow children to indulge in their own explorations and investigations. As Helm and Katz (2001) point out, the documentation collected throughout the life of a project is displayed alongside or in place of an end product. In effect, the process detailed in the documentation becomes the product.

For a more detailed explanation of the planning, observation and assessment process, with examples of documentation from a full-scale project, see the second part of this book.

External commitments

Projects can be flexible according to the various commitments and constraints of practitioners and settings. It is common practice for practitioners teaching in a school setting to be restricted by the wider school timetable. For instance, the children might be required to attend an assembly once a week; they might only have access to computers in a shared suite, available on certain days; and they may have to eat lunch in a cafeteria at a particular time. Practitioners in smaller private settings may also be subject to certain time restrictions such as regular swimming or music lessons or a weekly visit to the library. In this case it is advisable to set up a provocation or begin a project on a day that is free from any external commitment so that the children are able to become fully involved without interruption. If later in the project an interesting occurrence is unavoidably interrupted, it is a good idea to make a note so that it can be revisited at a more convenient time.

Disruption to routines

Children need "routines and information" (Nutbrown, 2006, p.28). Routines make children feel safe. Knowing what to expect when and where enables children to make sense of their day and week. However, it is just as vital for children to experience unexpected events and surprises. This is important, firstly because it is such experiences that encourage creativity and imaginative thought, and secondly because the real world is not always predictable. Running a project does not mean that the daily routine needs to be completely disrupted. The skeletal routine of everyday events, such as morning greetings, phonics sessions, lunch times, rest times and story times can be kept in place. However, there is a possibility that the spontaneous nature of a provocation might cause a break from the daily routine, and when this happens it will help if the children are kept informed about why and helped to adjust (Nutbrown, 2006). The project featured in the second part of this book is a working example of this. It was planned to fit around the pre-existing timetable of regular activities and the daily routine continued as far as possible without disruption.

Developing a disposition for learning

We know that young children are more likely to invest their energies, ideas and initiative when they are trusted to take responsibility and are making their own decisions and choices, rather than simply responding to adult requirements. (Dowling, 2008, p.14)

Montessori believed that children are born with a desire to find out more. It is the task of early years practitioners to harness and nurture this innate interest and thirst for knowledge. Providing opportunities for children to find out more about what interests them will result in their developing a positive attitude towards learning. Steiner and Froebel suggested that children who are intrinsically motivated are more likely to exercise self-discipline, an attribute that helps people to meet goals and succeed in their endeavours (Bruce, 2005). If practitioners find themselves needing rewards in order to persuade children to undertake certain tasks, it is likely that these tasks are inappropriate and this will lead to repeated failure (Katz and Chard, 2000). Csikszentmihayli (1992) explains that such failure impacts upon children's desire to learn and any potential they may have to become enthusiastic life-long learners. As Vygotsky pointed out, a child can only "imitate" a teacher and fully understand a task if operating "within her developmental level" (1978, p.88).

Therefore, planning for children's learning should start with what they "can do, rather than what they cannot do" (Bruce, 2005, p.50). The Welsh Foundation Phase Framework is littered with the word "appropriate" and states, "the development of children's self-image and feelings of self-worth and self-esteem are at the core of this phase" (DCELLS, 2008a, p.4). Additionally, the EYFS asks early years practitioners to help children feel "secure and confident" in their learning by having "realistic expectations" about what they can do (DCSF, 2007, Principles into Practice Card 4.2). **Katz and Chard suggest that this is possible by using the project approach, which focuses upon "learning goals" rather than "performance goals" (2000, p.42).** They explain that children judged on how well they do at particular tasks are reluctant to seek a challenge in case they fail. On the other hand, children judged on how much they can find out about something are

The project approach focuses upon learning goals. The aim of a project is to undertake an in-depth investigation to find out more. There are no right or wrong answers

New Zealand's early years curriculum places emphasis upon learning basic concepts that lay foundations for future learning

eager to take on a challenge and learn something new. This is because there are no unrealistic expectations placed upon them. As a result failure is seen as part of the learning process and not something to be ashamed or afraid of.

Donaldson (1978) pointed out that regular failure inevitably leads to low self-esteem. She suggested that children who are offered rewards are motivated by the teacher rather than the task. Usually the task is too difficult for many children and those who fail watch the others around them succeed and receive rewards. As a result these children deem themselves as failures. Maslow placed self-esteem forth in his hierarchy of basic needs. He suggested that children who are bolstered in this respect develop feelings of "self-confidence, worth, strength, capability and adequacy". On the other hand, if a child's self-esteem is damaged this will lead to feelings of "inferiority, of weakness and of helplessness" (1943, p.382). Furthermore, if children are worried or concerned that they are failing to meet expectations they may feel anxious and children who are anxious or worried have difficulties learning (Isaacs, 1930).

This philosophy on learning can be considered in relation to how literacy teaching is approached in early years provision in Britain. It has been suggested that accountability measures such as league tables and the EYFS Profile have created a tick-box culture that has contributed towards an unbalanced curriculum in favour of literacy and numeracy (Alexander, 2010). All four British early years curriculum documents have detailed and comprehensive sections relating to the teaching of literacy skills. The EYFS has been criticized for its focus upon literacy and the inclusion of a number of unrealistic communication, language and literacy early learning goals (Scott, 2008; Tickell, 2011). Downward pressure to prepare children for meeting the requirements of the National Curriculum for key stage one has resulted in some early years practices that are viewed as inappropriate (Hurst, 1994; Palmer, 2005). Practitioners in Britain vary in their opinions about what is developmentally appropriate for the children in their care and policy makers are constantly readdressing which approaches to promote. Children are taught literacy using a range of methods depending upon the type of setting they attend. This might include repeated drill-style repetitive phonics sessions, guided reading, shared writing, handwriting practice, puzzles, games and imaginative play. Toward the end of the foundation stage especially, children are increasingly required to participate in more structured academic activity, such as regular phonics sessions and more formal literacy and numeracy instruction (Palmer, 2005; Bayley, 2007; Defries, 2008).

Early years curriculum models such as New Zealand's Te Whāriki and the Swedish Curriculum for the Preschool promote alternative approaches that put much more emphasis on laying solid foundations that children can build upon and use when they enter more formal education later. This is evident in the structure of the Te Whāriki curriculum framework, which is divided into strands – well-being, belonging, contribution, communication and exploration – that focus upon the holistic personal, social and emotional development of the child, rather than academic, subject-based knowledge. In terms of literacy, the document puts emphasis upon the development of verbal and non-verbal

communication skills and promotes practice that helps children to "develop concepts" of reading, writing and language. This recognition that **children need a conceptual basis before embarking upon formal learning** is reinforced in the aim that by the age of five, children "are likely to...be ready to consolidate concepts about print" and have some "experience with some of the technology and resources for mathematics, reading, and writing" (New Zealand Ministry of Education, 1996, pp.73 and 79). Additionally, the underlying principle of the Swedish curriculum is that meaning is at the heart of learning and children create meaning through communication and play (Organisation for Economic Co-operation and Development, 2004). The development and learning strand of the curriculum acknowledges, "activities should promote play, creativity and enjoyment of learning". Also, like in New Zealand, there is a focus in Sweden on the development of "concepts" in literacy with goals including the "ability to play with words, an interest

A child-centred pedagogy

The project approach helps children develop a disposition for learning

Intrinsic motivation	Focus on learning	Meaningful context

Children are interested and so want to learn. They are more likely to enjoy tasks and persevere	Children are not judged on performance. The aim is to learn and find out more	Projects give children a meaningful context through which to learn and practise academic skills

How the project approach helps children develop a disposition for learning

Demonstrating a positive disposition to learn and use literacy skills: an example

Name suggestion basket

Earlier on in the term the class teacher had set up a suggestions box for children to write and post possible names for some baby stick insects. Drawing on this experience, they suggested that the same was done for the creature that had hatched from the cocoon. A basket with some pencils and slips of paper was left out for the children to leave their suggestions. These included 'Bloowi', 'Bloey', 'Cudi, 'Bugby' and 'Antianti'. At the end of the week Beckham was chosen to dip into the basket and he chose 'Tom'.

A letter from America

It was noted by the children that Tom bared an uncanny resemblance to Flik from the animated film *A Bug's Life*. Tom explained that Flik was in fact his uncle. The children were concerned that Uncle Flik might be worried and so decided to write him a letter to explain where his nephew was to reassure him that he was all right. The letters were sent to Uncle Flik's home 'Ant Hill' in America and a week later the children received a response, prompting them to reply.

Projects provide a meaningful context forlearning that encourages young children to want to read and write

Stories

Some children mentioned that they had books at home related to Flik and *A Bug's Life*. They were asked to bring these in and they were shared with the class.

in the written language and an understanding of symbols" (Swedish Ministry of Education and Science, 1998, pp. 9 and 10).

It is examples such as these that the Welsh Assembly Government looked to in its re-evaluation of early years education that led to a foundation phase that includes children up to the age of seven (National Assembly for Wales, 2003). It should be noted that the importance of helping young children to develop self-confidence early on, as well as the need to establish basic communication skills before embarking upon learning more formal literacy learning, is recognised by Dame Tickell in her recent review of the EYFS. Dame Tickell recommends that personal, social and emotional development, communication and language, and physical development be identified as "prime areas of learning" (2011, p.6). These, she suggests, need to

be "securely in place" to enable the child to progress in the other specific areas of learning, identified as literacy, mathematics, understanding the world, and expressive arts and design (2011, p.96).

Helm and Katz (2001) highlight the benefits of project work for providing an age-appropriate meaningful context for the learning and teaching of literacy and numeracy skills to young children. They explain that if children know the purpose of learning certain literacy and numeracy skills they will be more positive about doing so and there should be no need for rewards as incentives.
The example above demonstrates the wide range of literacy activities that were triggered by the cocoon provocation. The appearance of the creature gave the children a legitimate purpose for wanting to write. The creature needed a name and a democratic way of choosing this was to collect suggestions and pick

from them. The provocation also provided a context through which the children could learn about the purpose of letter writing and experience genuine excitement when receiving a letter in response to those they had sent. The use of a familiar character from a film within the children's frame of reference also spurred them on to want to share their own related books and stories from home.

Katz and Chard (2000) promote the project approach because it focuses upon learning goals and provides a meaningful context for introducing academic skills. Furthermore, they suggest project work helps children to "become experts in their own learning" as they make choices about the level of challenge they wish to undertake (2000, p.15). They explain the open-ended nature of project work enables children

---

The ability to empathise: an example

When the creature's head first appeared, the children discussed whether he should be brought down out of the cocoon.

Hannah: Might have to see if it's awake or not and if he's asleep you should leave him there.

Grania: I think if he's asleep you should leave him there.

Elliot: If you just take the thing that it's in off the wall then we could look at it. If we take it out then it will lose its home.

Cameron suggested the children should ask, "Please can I show the little boys and girls you?"

Gaby: It might miss its mum and dad if you take it out of its home.

Ellie: Just leave it.

Joey: If we take him down he might be scared. If we leave him up there he might not be scared. He might feel cold if we take the paper off.

Jessica: He might be scared because there are so many children.

Jasmin: Its eyes are open. It's waking up. I think we need to make it go back to sleep. We could sing it a sleepy song.

---

of different ages and abilities to participate according to what knowledge and skills they have to offer. It is their success in these endeavours that then spurs them on to stretch themselves further. Stead agrees: "Collaborative projects give endless opportunities for children to choose learning experiences at the right level, and to progress from easy activities to more challenging ones" (2009, p.43). It is a combination of these features of the project approach that promote a positive disposition for learning.

Personal, social and emotional development

A child-centred curriculum should value personal, social and emotional skills and regard these as equal in value to academic skills (New Zealand Ministry of Education, 1996). Wood and Attfield (2005) explain that promoting social skills is important because they help children to:

- Work with others and attempt to solve any personal problems that might impact upon a working relationship;

- Develop empathy and understand the views and feelings of others;

- Develop self-control.

Helm and Katz credit the project approach with helping children to develop a range of personal, social and emotional skills. They explain that in-depth study of a topic results in children becoming "meaniwngfully engaged" and emotionally involved, which spurs them on to want to achieve and learn (2001, p.5). They further point to research demonstrating a link between hands-on active learning experiences and better-developed social skills. The example on the left demonstrates that projects and provocations can appeal to young children's sensibilities to such an extent that they display high levels of emotional literacy and understanding of others. The four and five-year-old children in this example were especially worried about scaring the creature and it was decided that he should be left in his cocoon until he was obviously ready to come out. This demonstration of compassion and empathy for the creature was unexpected and illustrates the power of such an exercise.

Respected and included: an example

The visual nature of the cocoon provocation appealed to the imagination of four-year-old Finn, who has motor difficulties and is profoundly deaf. Although he has cochlear implants and knows some sign language, he finds it extremely difficult to follow whole class discussion and is unable to fully participate.

When the creature began to break out of the cocoon, there was such alarm and excitement that it was decided to bring everyone together and divide into talk partners to discuss what was happening. With the help of his support assistant and the visual stimulus of the cocoon, Finn was able to take part in whole class discussion for the first time. He pointed to the cocoon and said 'green one' to his partner. He signed 'broke' and said 'blue', signing 'tiger' before adding, 'it's a cat!'

The children's emotional involvement and engagement with the cocoon provocation led them to demonstrate high levels of emotional literacy and empathy

Helm and Katz (2001) also suggest that the project approach helps children to develop as democratic citizens. They explain that the project approach promotes a positive disposition for work, presenting children with the opportunity to put sustained effort into projects that involve in-depth investigation. **Through group project work children learn about societal interdependence and how to value the differences in others (Katz and Chard, 2000). Children develop social dispositions that equip them for living and working with others as they grow older and integrate themselves into adult society.**

Everyone included

Bredekamp and Copple highlight the importance of "creating a caring community of learners" within early years settings. They explain that this is accomplished by providing "meaningful tasks" for children to work on in groups and emphasize that such tasks should cater "to individual differences in abilities" so that children with special educational needs are "included in the classroom socially and intellectually" (1997, pp.123 and 125). The EYFS places value on the "diversity of individuals" and states, "all children are entitled to

enjoy a full life in conditions which will help them take part in society" (DCSF, 2007, Principles into Practice Card 1.2). This is reminiscent of the Reggio Emilia Approach where all children are viewed as powerful, autonomous individuals that are full of potential. This philosophy allows for the natural inclusion of children with special educational needs and values the difference they bring to the community (Gilman, 2007).

The visual nature of the cocoon provocation ensured that the imaginations of all children were captured and they felt able to contribute regardless of ability.

The provocation gave practitioners a unique insight into the extent of Finn's capabilities. As well as being relevant, his comments demonstrated information processing skills as he described what he could see, and reasoning skills as he formed an opinion as to what might be inside the cocoon. The cocoon provocation demonstrates how it is possible to plan according to the children's interests and deliver curriculum subjects in a playful, inclusive and child-friendly manner. Using the project approach does not mean neglecting academic teaching but approaching it in an alternative way. There are high expectations of all children as competent learners who are interested and willing to learn. **Exciting projects motivate children and provide a meaningful context through which to teach important skills**.

Key points

■ **The project approach is a child-centred pedagogy that builds upon the interests of the children.**

■ **The project approach assumes a positive view of the child as a competent learner who is able to take an active role in their education.**

■ **Project work provides children with time and space to investigate and find out information for themselves.**

■ **Project work helps children to develop a positive disposition for learning. When involved in projects children are intrinsically motivated, making them more likely to persevere at difficult tasks.**

■ **The project approach places emphasis upon learning goals where the aim is to find out more. Children are not judged on performance or whether they get a task right or wrong.**

■ **Projects provide children with a meaningful context through which to learn and practice academic skills.**

Developmentally appropriate practice

This section features a provocation entitled frozen balloons, as an example of how the project approach can help early years practitioners to facilitate developmentally appropriate practice within their settings.

An appropriate and effective teaching approach

Quality learning is about three things: the child, the context in which learning takes place, and the knowledge and understanding which the child develops and learns. (Bruce, 2005, p.31)

Frozen Balloons

Large Town Community Primary School, Jersey*

This provocation was set up in a 40-place nursery at a primary school in Jersey. It was a short project, lasting just two days and involved working with small groups to investigate melting ice. Although the adult was the instigator of this project, the children were involved from the very start, helping to set it up and following the entire process as it unfolded.

On the first day the class teacher took one group at a time and showed them a number of deflated balloons in various shapes and sizes. She told the children that each of the balloons was to be filled with water and frozen. Showing the children the size of a balloon's opening and neck, she explained that they could choose some small items to put into the balloons, i.e. tiny objects or colourings and invited them to make suggestions.

Each group chose two balloons and the teacher helped as the children worked in pairs to squeeze a variety of small objects including shells, LEGO and glass pebbles inside with the aid of a funnel. Food colouring, paint and glitter were also added for effect before the children assisted in filling the balloons with water straight from a tap – a fiddly and very messy task! The children then helped to carry the balloons and put them into a chest freezer over night.

The following day, the balloons were taken from the freezer two at a time and placed in the water tray. Children were brought over in groups to closely inspect them periodically throughout the day as the ice melted, the rubber skins peeled away and the objects inside were revealed. Two adults observed all the time, asking questions to provoke thought, recording the children's comments and taking photographs of their expressions.

*All names have been changed in the interests of confidentiality.

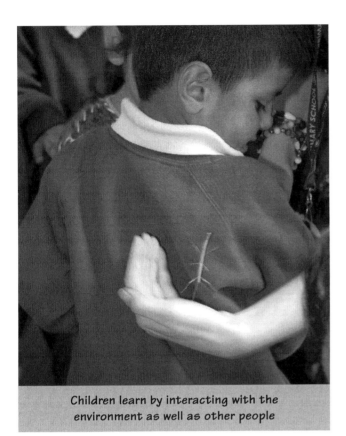

Children learn by interacting with the environment as well as other people

The Effective Provision of Preschool Education (EPPE) project established a link between good quality early experience and later educational achievement. In this research, effective pedagogical strategies outlined included a balance of child and adult-initiated activities and the use of play as a "basis of instructive learning" (Siraj-Blatchford et al, 2004, p.vi). Furthermore, the Researching Effective Pedagogy in the Early Years (REPEY) researchers recommended that an effective approach constituted a balance between "teacher-directed, programmed learning" and children being "provided with 'free' access to a range of instructive learning environments in which adults support children's learning" (Siraj-Blatchford et al, 2002a, p.4). In addition, the related Study of Pedagogical Effectiveness in Early Learning (SPEEL) placed emphasis upon building on children's capabilities, needs, interests, experiences and learning styles. It recommended practitioners "ensure time is available for children to fully explore and extend concepts, ideas and interests and complete tasks to their own satisfaction" (Moyles et al, 2002, p.54).

These research findings support the view that **children learn by interacting with the environment around them as well as other people, assimilating these experiences into their own "mental structures" in order to further develop knowledge and understanding (Howe and Davies, 2005, p.155).** The frozen balloons provocation is an example of how the project approach can help practitioners deliver an educational experience in line with this view and the above research recommendations.

The use of play in instructive learning

In 1967 Plowden acknowledged that play had a key role as a motivating medium through which children develop knowledge and understanding of the world (CACE, 1967). Current research into how young children learn also supports this idea of playfulness supporting learning. Howard and McInnes point out that children make "play-work distinctions" (2010, p.14). They explain that many children view play as child-controlled, physical, fun, easy and focused upon a process. This is as opposed to work, which is often seen as compulsory, hard and focused upon a product. Howard and McInnes refer to research involving asking children to solve puzzles while under various practice conditions. These studies found that the children who tackled a puzzle in a playful context (for example voluntarily on the floor without an adult), appeared to be more involved, motivated and positive about the task. This is in contrast to those children, who attempted the task in a more formal context (for example at a table at the request of an adult), who were observed to be less motivated and engaged.

The value of play has been particularly attributed to the development of scientific learning. Howe and Davies (2005) point out that play offers children the opportunity to develop scientific concepts and knowledge in a wide variety of ways: "Every time children pick up, squash, slide or roll objects, arrange them in lines or build them into towers, they are exercising those parts of their brains concerned with spatial and logical-mathematical thought... they are being scientists." (Howe and Davies, 2005, p.156).

They explain that children's spontaneous play can provide a context for practitioners to teach scientific concepts by sensitively joining children's play to ask questions and offer explanations. However, they also suggest that playful opportunities for science

---

Kinaesthetic learning – touching and doing: an example

"Cold! It makes your fingers hurt," said Emma.

Bernard touched each balloon, getting blue paint on his hands. "Paint! Paint!" he cried.

"It feels like it's melted. Hey, it's rea...lly cold!" said Jason.

"It's very slimy. It's wet as well. Why is there no water? Did that balloon burst?" asked Christopher.

Visual learning – seeing and reading: an example

As the ice melted puddles of water formed at the bottom of the tray and the hidden objects inside were gradually revealed.

"The ice has come out. Looks like an ice-cream," said Lionel.

Christopher noticed the melting water in the bottom of the tray. "Look, it's coming up," he said.

"It's cold and there's something inside!" cried Grania.

"It's a football – like a football," said Gemma.

Andrew looked closely at a balloon and noticed it "twinkle".

---

exploration can be "planned" or "structured" by adults (Howe and Davies, 2005, p.159). Wood and Attfield also point out the positive relationship between play and learning should provide a basis for an appropriate early years pedagogical model: "...early childhood specialists need to value play through creating appropriate contexts and conditions for learning, which promote a continuum between play and work, and incorporate playful approaches to teaching and learning" (2005, p.17).

The frozen balloons provocation is an example of how practitioners can provide a basis for instructive learning by setting up a playful, yet structured context for children to engage in sensory exploration and experiment with scientific concepts. It was planned in the knowledge that **young children learn best when interacting with the environment through sensory exploration and play.**

Building on children's capabilities, interests, experiences and learning styles

The *Excellence and Enjoyment* document states that children should be helped to "develop understanding through enquiry" and that this is accomplished by "matching teaching techniques and strategies to a range of learning styles" (DfES, 2003, p.29). The following observations demonstrate how the frozen balloons provocation appealed to all of the senses and as a result encompassed a range of learning styles.

Auditory learning – listening and speaking: an example

Freddie peeled the balloon skin off the green balloon. "Cold," he said. "There's water in it."
"It's sticky as well," Charlie added.

"Can I touch it?" Shelagh asked. "It's very cold."
"They got cold in the freezer," replied Ivy.

"I like this," said Jennifer. "It's water."
"It's not water," replied Damien.
"It's freezing cold," said Jennifer.
"It's orange," said Damien.
"No it's gold. The colour is gold," Jennifer replied.

When the children first encountered the balloons they immediately reached out and touched them, peeling away pieces of rubber and stretching it with their fingers. It was through this physical interaction that they were learning about the properties of frozen water. The visual nature of this provocation enabled all of the children to witness the melting process, making it easier to understand.

The children's conversations in the example opposite show how the provocation acted as a stimulus for comment and debate. The children were expanding and developing each other's knowledge and understanding as they listened and responded to each other's observational comments.

As already mentioned, a basic premise of the project approach is that learning should start with the interests of the children, as it is the children's curiosity that drives their learning. Although the frozen balloons provocation was adult-initiated, the children were involved from the very beginning, taking an active role and making decisions about how it was set up. This grabbed their interest, which had a motivational effect that highlighted their intellectual abilities. **The provocation's playful and practical nature built upon the children's capabilities, making it a developmentally appropriate way of introducing basic scientific concepts to nursery-age children.** Furthermore, the open-ended nature of this provocation provided for differentiation by outcome

and practitioners had the opportunity to closely observe each child individually, assess their level of understanding and identify future learning goals.

Shared control between children and adults

One of the most challenging aspects of early years practice is deciding to what extent practitioners should control and plan the activities of the children in their care. National early years guidance recommends planning for "a mixture of child-initiated play, supported by adults [and] focused learning, with adults guiding the learning through playful, rich experiential activities" (DCSF, 2009, p.5). Featherstone and Featherstone suggest that an effective balance between adult-led and child-initiated activities is "roughly equal" (2008, p.4). A balance of shared control between adults and children is also advocated by Lindon (2008), who further suggests that "enjoyable adult-initiated experiences" are those that children are able to join

---

Adult-initiated group work as a vehicle for promoting learning: an example

The children were asked to choose some items that they would like to put inside the balloons with the aid of a funnel.

Terrence liked the idea of putting a toy car inside. The teacher held the car next to the opening of the balloon.

Teacher: How do you think we might be able to get this car inside the balloon?
Terrence: It's stretchy.
Teacher: Do you think the opening will stretch over the car?
Terrence: Yes.
Teacher: Shall we give it a try?

The teacher pulled the mouth of the balloon open and tried to stretch it over the car without succeeding.

Teacher: I'm not sure that it will stretch far enough.

Terrence: We need something small.

Olive and Jacqueline chose to fill a balloon with rice and added some blue food colouring.

Teacher: How do you think you might be able to get the rice inside the balloon?
Olive: I don't know.
Teacher: Can you pour it in?
Jacqueline: It's stuck together.
Olive: You have to stick your finger in.

Jacqueline stretched the balloon opening with her fingers and Olive tried to pour some rice in. It spilled over the sides.

Teacher: I think your fingers might be getting in the way. Do you know what this is for? [Holds up a funnel].
Olive: You can pour water in it.
Teacher: Or rice. [Pours rice].

The teacher stretched the balloon opening over the funnel. Jacqueline then held the funnel while Olive poured some rice inside.

---

and then take over while the adult withdraws and relinquishes control.

The frozen balloons provocation is an example of how projects help practitioners to strike a balance and teach children while giving them some control over their own learning. In this case, the practitioners initially thought of the idea for the provocation. They then shared control of setting it up with the children by asking them for ideas and involving them in the process. The children were then given space to explore their frozen creations without adult direction or control.

The REPEY research illustrates the importance of a balance of control between children and adults. Here it was found that good quality interactions are more likely to occur when children are interacting with an adult or peer in small groups, or in a one-to-one situation (Siraj-Blatchford et al, 2002a). On the strength of this, Siraj-Blatchford recommends that practitioners plan to provide opportunities "to extend child-initiated play as well as teacher-initiated group work, as both of these have been found to be important vehicles for promoting learning" (2010, p.158). The examples from the frozen balloons provocation on page 25 demonstrate how the project approach can help practitioners to do this. The children worked in pairs while setting up the provocation. This allowed the practitioner to observe more easily, listen more clearly to their conversations and follow their threads of thinking before deciding when it was best to intervene.

In each example, the adult used open questioning to encourage the children to actively consider the task. The adult then assisted the children in trying out their ideas before offering a solution. The children later investigated the balloons in small groups, which enabled them to talk more easily and freely together as they shared ideas and observations. When practitioners plan for such opportunities it is more likely that children

---

Developmentally appropriate practice

Project work provides for shared control between children and adults

Adult-initiated activity	Child-initiated activity	Researching Effective Pedagogy in the Early Years (REPEY)
Adults set up projects and provocations	Children take over the activity and this leads to their own initiated activities	Good quality instructions are more likely to occur in one-to-one situations (child-initiated play) and small groups (adult-initiated group work)

How the project approach allows for the shared control of learning

---

Children need hands-on playful experiences to develop
knowledge and understanding of basic concepts

Project work involves a balance of
adult-led and child-initiated activities

will engage in good quality interactions that help to develop their cognitive skills. A more detailed account of how project work promotes learning through social interaction is provided in relation to the where is George? provocation on page 33.

The project approach provides for a balance of adult-led and child-initiated learning. Provocations are set up by adults to stimulate the interest and imaginations of the children and this leads to spin-off activities that are initiated by the children. This is more clearly shown in the child-initiated activities that resulted from the cocoon provocation described on page 12.

Active learning

Active learning is defined as learning in which the child, by acting on objects and interacting with people, ideas and events, constructs new understanding. (Hohmann and Weikart, 2002, quoted in Holt, 2007, p.13)

It has already been established that children have a natural urge to explore their environment and investigate phenomena. Physical exploration of

objects as a way of learning has been endorsed in the work of many early years pioneers who have influenced early education in Britain. In the eighteenth century Pestalozzi recognised the child's need to learn through concrete experience. The children in his experimental schools in Switzerland were taught using practical methods that aimed to develop understanding of concepts and ideas. It was his belief that it is only once children have grasped these understandings that they are ready to move onto more formal learning (Pound, 2008). Building upon Pestalozzi's ideas, Froebel placed even greater emphasis upon physical exploration and play and especially outdoor learning. He explained that children reflect upon their learning through play, which "helps them to grasp and try out their learning in concrete ways" (Bruce, 2005, p.20). Montessori and Steiner also recognised the value of giving children opportunities to learn through practical and meaningful experiences, as did Isaacs, who, when recalling her experience at the Malting House School during the 1920s wrote, "we wanted to stimulate the active inquiry of the children themselves, rather than to 'teach' them" (Isaacs, 1930, p.17).

Like in the past, it is now generally agreed and proven through research that young children should be exposed to "direct and immediate" learning experiences and be provided "opportunities to be active and take the initiative to learn" (Siraj-Blatchford et al, 2002b, p.31). Bredekamp and Copple suggest that developmentally appropriate practice for three to five year olds involves practitioners allocating time for "concrete learning experiences" that "promote their interest, engagement and learning". They explain that allowing children to be hands-on enables them to find things out for themselves and "experiment with cause-and-effect relationships" (1997, p.126). This is a central principle of a number of renowned and respected approaches to early childhood education – including Montessori, Reggio Emilia, High/Scope and Steiner Waldorf – in which it is believed that suitable early learning practice constitutes "active feeling, touching, exploring, imitating… doing" (Nicol, 2007, p.7). Katz and Chard believe that a child's innate "disposition to make sense of experience" is at risk of being lost if not used (2000, p.35). They explain that children given the opportunity to investigate and obtain information for themselves will gain a deeper understanding as well as confidence in themselves as proficient learners. **Support for an active approach to teaching and learning is evident in all current British early years curricula, within which it is generally agreed that young children learn through first-hand investigation and physical exploration** (DCSF, 2007; Scottish Executive, 2007; DCELLS, 2008a):

> *Young children learn best when learning is interactive, practical and enjoyable for both children and teachers… [and when they] have opportunities to be actively involved in practical, open-ended and challenging learning experiences that encourage creativity. (CCEA, 2006, p.4)*

Project work provides a wealth of opportunities for active learning as the extract on the right from the frozen balloons learning story demonstrates.

The children helped to set up the provocation by choosing familiar everyday objects to put inside the balloons and added some extra ingredients with the help of an adult. Allowing the children to help with the risky task of filling the balloons from a tap caused a great deal of anticipation and excitement. This was a thrilling hands-on way to find out size, volume and force, as well as an effective stimulus for the use of expressive and descriptive language. (For

---

Active involvement: an example

Christopher and Steven used a funnel to pour some rice into a balloon and added some red food colouring. Another group decided to use glass pebbles. Some were clear and others were frosted. "This one's darker red," said Jack. The children looked at the pebbles once they were inside the balloon. "They're big," said Kirstie.

Charlotte held the balloon while the teacher filled it with water from the tap. "It's getting round," said Olive. "Don't squeeze it or it'll pop!" warned Jacqueline.

The teacher tried to fill another balloon but the water forced it off the tap, spurting out all over the place. "It splashed the wall!" cried Steven.

Darren and Emma chose to fill a long blue balloon with glitter. As the teacher was carrying the full balloon to the water tray she lost her grip and glittery water squirted out everywhere causing everyone to scream and laugh.

---

examples of children learning and using literacy skills see the cocoon provocation on page 19.)

Actively constructing knowledge and understanding

Piaget believed that children build knowledge though interactions with the environment around them (Mooney, 2000). In this constructivist view, children are not seen as empty vessels that need filling with ready-made knowledge, but rather competent learners who are able to construct their own knowledge. He contended that children should be allowed to discover information for themselves through their own investigations of the world and described learning as an internal process whereby children perform actions and reflect upon them. Children investigate things physically and then internalise the knowledge they gain from this experience (Bruce, 2005). Adults can support this by providing an enabling environment and scaffolding the learning process with questions and conversation, but they cannot actually create the thinking process for the child.

Piaget's emphasis on the importance of learning through experience is shared by the influential theorist Jerome Bruner:

We teach a subject not to produce little living libraries on that subject, but rather to get a student to think mathematically for himself, to consider matters as an historian does, to take part in the process of knowledge-getting. Knowing is a process not a product. (Bruner, 1966, p.72)

Children do not arrive in early years settings as blank slates: from birth they have been investigating the world and developing their own knowledge. It is important to encourage children to share their ideas and build upon them as they strive to find out more. The example below from the frozen balloons provocation exemplifies this point.

The children in the example below were clearly drawing upon their previous experience of balloons bursting when too full. Jason, especially, showed

understanding of the concept of filling something until it is full. It is possible he gained such knowledge while playing with containers in the water tray in the past. In the second example on page 30 David demonstrates an understanding of freezing. He understands that the balloon has been filled with cold water and after being in the freezer has become ice. His comment that he "sucks ice" shows that he is drawing on personal experience to make these assumptions. It is clear that he has knowledge of drinking an iced drink.

Featherstone and Featherstone (2008) describe the relationship between knowledge, skills and understanding. They explain that children build knowledge through subject teaching, topics or themes. Children learn to apply this knowledge through the acquisition of skills, which are developed through practise. It is this practical experience and experimentation that helps children to develop understanding.

This is further illustrated by Katz and Chard (2000), who explain the importance of active learning in terms of how children acquire knowledge. They set out two types of knowledge: behavioural and representational.

During a project adults support learning by providing an enabling environment and scaffolding children's thinking

Building upon experience: an example

While filling a balloon with water the teacher did not turn the tap off in time and it burst.

"It splashed!" Jason cried. "There was too much water in it!"

"It popped!" shouted Charlotte.

Imogen touched a water filled balloon. "It's cold," she said.

"Yeah, because it's got cold water in it," said David.

The following day the balloons were retrieved from the freezer.

"They're freezing," said David. "It's ice. I suck ice."

Hands-on learning experiences help children to develop an understanding of how things work. It is by internalising this behavioural knowledge that children develop representational knowledge, which enables them to explain the events they witness and observe

- **Behavioural knowledge:** what a child needs to carry out an action or behaviour; Katz and Chard use the example of a child being able to navigate through her house.

- **Representational knowledge:** what a child needs to be able to explain or describe the action or behaviour; so in the case of this example, the child being able to represent her house in the form of a map.

It is Katz and Chard's assertion that children are traditionally taught representational knowledge first. This means that they have difficulty processing and understanding the abstract representation because they do not have the behavioural knowledge base to do so: "An appropriate curriculum first strengthens and extends children's behavioural knowledge and then helps them to employ a variety of abstract representations directly related to it" (2000, p.29).

Developing behavioural knowledge: an example

Scientific concepts such as freezing and melting are difficult for young children to understand when presented to them in an abstract way. The children in this example were actively involved in the physical process of filling balloons with water, taking them to a freezer, collecting them the following day once frozen and then observing them as they melted in a warm classroom. Even then, some children were struggling to understand what had actually happened:

Edward tried to peel the balloon skin off the ice.

Edward: It won't come out! I want it to come out!
Teacher: The ice is so cold that the balloon skin is stuck to it. Touch the ice with your fingers; they might stick to it too.
Edward: What is it?
Teacher: It's ice. When we put the balloons in the freezer they became very cold. When water is very cold it freezes and goes hard – it turns into ice.

Christopher looked at a balloon shaped piece of ice with the rubber peeled off:

Christopher: Why is there no water?
Teacher: This is the water [touches the ice]. You feel it.
Christopher: [Touches the ice] It's very slimy. It's wet as well.
Teacher: Yes, it's wet because it is water. When we put the water in the freezer it got very cold and went hard and turned into ice. Now it is getting warmer the ice is melting and becoming runny water again.
Christopher: Did that balloon burst?
Teacher: Yes I think so. When the water froze it expanded … got bigger, and could not fit in the balloon anymore so the balloon skin broke.

Project work provides the opportunity for children to develop behavioural knowledge first through active investigation. It then helps children to develop representational knowledge through the process of presenting and reflecting upon their findings. The examples on the left from the frozen balloons provocation demonstrate this.

The children's active participation was a lot more valuable than any verbal or pictorial explanation the practitioner could offer. Even with the help the children's comments demonstrate the difficulty they were having understanding the freezing and melting process. However, they were beginning to acquire the behavioural knowledge that they needed in order to later develop representational knowledge. In this case, the practitioner helped the children to consolidate their behavioural knowledge and begin to acquire some representational knowledge by showing them a learning story compiled from photographs and observations of the children. The learning story featured photographs of the whole provocation from start to finish. This allowed the children to look back at how they filled the balloons with water, placed them in a freezer and then investigated them. The story contained comments and questions made by the children throughout. The children were able to re-live their concrete experience of freezing and melting and reflect upon it in an abstract way when it was represented in the learning story. For an example of a learning story see the 'all about eggs' story on the accompanying CD.

A playful and active approach to teaching and learning is supported by all four British early years curricula. The EYFS states that children "learn at their highest level" through play and "physical and mental challenges" (DCSF, 2007, Principles into Practice Cards 4.1 and 4.2). This is seconded by the Northern Ireland Curriculum, which promotes an "interactive" and "practical" approach to learning (CCEA, 2007, p.9) The Welsh Foundation Phase Framework also promotes active learning and describes play as a 'very serious business' (DCELLS, 2008a, p.6). What's more, Scotland has produced specific guidance on the benefits of active learning (Scottish Executive, 2007).

The frozen balloons provocation is an example of how the practical nature of project work makes it a developmentally appropriate approach to teaching young children. This helps to ensure that

they have the best possible chance at succeeding in their endeavors, which in turn motivates them to want to learn more. **The project approach might be described as a more natural way to teach young children, enabling them to draw upon personal experience and follow their own individual learning path, and allowing them to play and participate at their own developmental level.**

Key points

- **The project approach encompasses developmentally appropriate practices promoted by early years pioneers, such as Montessori, Froebel, Steiner and Piaget, as well as contemporary research including EPPE, REPEY and SPEEL.**

- **Projects and provocations promote learning through play. Children learn in a structured yet playful context.**

- **The open-ended nature of project work allows for children to participate according to their own individual interests, aptitudes and abilities.**

- **Project work provides for shared control between children and adults, which leads to better quality interaction and learning.**

- **Projects and provocations promote active learning. Children acquire knowledge and develop skills though practical hands-on experience, leading to greater understanding.**

Learning together

The project approach involves group learning experiences that lead to the social construction of knowledge and understanding, and provide an ideal arena for promoting sustained shared thinking. Children use communication skills to interact with others, make sense of their experiences and process information. Practitioners encourage children to use a range of thinking skills by joining in with the discussion and debate, and posing questions for children to consider. The where is George? provocation featured in this section is an example of how this works in practice.

Where is George?

Horton Grange Primary School, Bradford

This provocation was set up in a reception class in an inner city community primary school in Bradford, where the majority of the 30 children speak English as an additional language. The provocation was planned to fit into a class topic about people who help us and was triggered with the appearance of a letter from the resident class puppet George explaining that he had "gone away".

In this case the children were immediately gathered on the carpet to listen as Ms. Matthews, the class teacher, read the letter out loud. Initially, the children were stunned into silence until one little boy announced "George gone away!" Ms. Matthews then asked, "Where do you think he has gone?" The children began to speculate as to his whereabouts and embarked upon a search of the classroom.

One child suggested that they call the police and a large-scale missing person investigation began. The practitioners set up an incident room and provided role-play police officer uniforms. "Missing" posters were displayed around the classroom.

It was decided that the community police should be invited to come into the setting to give the children an opportunity to ask for some help and advice. The officers took away a poster to display at the station, said they would file a "missing puppet report", promising to keep the children informed of any developments. Following this, a photograph of George sitting on a park bench near a river was sent to the class, prompting yet more conjecture and debate.

After two weeks George was suddenly spotted hiding behind a classroom computer. After the initial excitement had died down the children began to wonder about how he might have found his way back and which type of transport he might have used. They suggested that he may need a clean, then set about welcoming him back, including him in their play, making him pictures and taking photographs of him.

George never did tell the children were he had been.

Developing communication skills

The ability to communicate is an essential life skill for all children and young people in the twenty-first century. It is at the core of all social interaction. With effective communication skills, children can engage and thrive. Without them, children will struggle to learn, achieve, make friends and interact with the world around them.
(Bercow, 2008, p.3)

Communication is central to the Reggio Emilia Approach, where children and adults learn from each other through collaborative project work that entails a constant process of reflection through sharing experiences and reviewing events. **The group work and discussion that arises from project work is seen as elemental in the children's development of communication and thinking skills (Thornton and Brunton, 2007).**

Communication skills are vital for learning. The acquisition, use and understanding of language provide a foundation that children can build upon to develop their knowledge and understanding in all areas (Clarke, 2007; Cooper, 2010). Wood and Attfield (2005) explain this process is called metacommunication. They explain that children need "language-rich experiences" because the acquisition of language is what makes it possible for children to formulate thoughts. Children use language to help process information and make sense of events and experiences. They then communicate this information to others, which consolidates their understanding.

In order for children to develop their communication skills, they need to be given the opportunity to engage in tasks that involve interaction (Cooper, 2010). Children are more likely to enter into and sustain meaningful conversation if the context and subject matter is important to them. Projects provide **a "purposeful,** meaningful, and authentic context in which children can sharpen their communicative skills" (Katz, 2002, quoted in Early Childhood Today, 2002). In the case of this example, George's disappearance was naturally perplexing, with the prospect of a search and investigation being a source of excitement for the children. The shocking event ignited their curiosity because it was a matter of importance to them and so all were interested and instantly engaged.

Katz and Chard further explain that children replay and act out familiar events from their own personal frames of reference as part of the knowledge-building process. They suggest that children all have their own "event knowledge" drawn from personal experience (2000, p.30). When involved in a project the children share their different event knowledge and learn from one another. It follows that projects should be based around subjects that the children will easily relate to and that they will have some depth of knowledge about. This is especially useful for children who have some form of communication delay or speak English as an additional language. Developing English speaking and listening skills is particularly important to the children in this example and George's disappearance triggered much discussion and debate.

An interesting project provides a meaningful context for children to practice their communication skills

The snippets of discussion in the example box below demonstrate how this provocation allowed each of the children to draw from their own personal frames of reference. This provided for ease of conversation, enabling them to share knowledge and express ideas verbally with confidence. The more confident speakers were given an opportunity to practice the language and widen their vocabulary, while the less confident were learning all the while they were listening to their peers.

Project work presents much opportunity for good quality adult-child interaction, which is credited as "a necessary prerequisite for excellence in early years practice" (Siraj-Blatchford, 2010, p.157). The where is George? provocation demonstrates how projects are an ideal vehicle for stimulating conversation and promoting language development. The exploratory process enabled the children to practice their speaking, listening, attention and comprehension skills, as they embarked upon their investigation as to where George had gone. Throughout the project that ensued, the children were required to clearly articulate their own thoughts and views, as well as actively listen to and engage with the ideas of others.

A social constructivist approach

Social constructivists believe children learn through interaction with others. In particular, Vygotsky highlighted the role of other people, society and culture in children's learning and development. He placed particular emphasis upon language and communication

---

Drawing from personal experience: an example

After searching and agreeing that George was not in the classroom the children were divided into groups to share ideas about where he might be:

Aishah: He's hiding.
Haroon: He's in the house.
Zeleha: I think he's outside.
Anis: He can't walk!
Isa: I think he's gone to another nursery.
Aliyah: I think he's gone to a big class.
Hamzah: Home away 'cos he's tired for a bit.

Learning together

Project work involves social interaction

Lev Vygotsky	Jerome Bruner

Children learn through play and conversation. They learn throuh social interaction with other people, society and culture	Introduced the term "scaffolding". Quality interaction between adults and children helps to improve understanding and further learning

The importance of social interaction to children's learning

and social exchange. He suggested that children develop ideas through play and conversation, furthering their learning through interaction with expert others. He described a child's potential in terms of her zone of proximal development. He suggested that an unassisted child is learning within her zone of actual development. However, help from others enables the child to extend her learning further, placing her in the zone of proximal development and giving her the potential to do more independently in the future; the zone of future development: "…what is the zone of proximal development today will be the actual developmental level tomorrow – that is, what a child can do with assistance today she will be able to do by herself tomorrow" (1978, p.87).

Bruner built upon Vygotsky's theory and introduced the term "scaffolding" (Wood et al, 1976, p.90). He describes joint involvement episodes whereby quality interaction between adults and children helps to

improve their understanding and further their learning. He believes that adults should carefully consider the stage of each individual child's development as well as their interests and target support accordingly. Such support should aim to give children agency enabling them to become confident and autonomous learners. Adults should gradually reduce the level of support, thereby transferring the control to the child and enabling them to become more independent. Broadhead considers this in terms of social and cooperative play between children. In her research she found that children introduce each other to different perspectives and that they "become experts for one another, scaffolding their own and their friends' learning experiences" (2004, p.123).

Rinaldi also stresses the importance of interaction and describes the Reggio pre-school as a "place of research" where practitioners and children work together on projects to co-create knowledge (2000, p.125). Communication between the child and her peers and adults is central to this approach and places the practitioner alongside the child as they collaborate to find meaning and explanation. She explains that children do not learn by having information simply fed to them. They need to take part in the knowledge building process through discussion, which involves reasoning, explaining and interpreting: "We thus consider knowledge to be a process of construction by the individual in relation with others, a true act of co-construction." (Rinaldi, 2000, p.125)

The EPPE project highlights the collaborative role of the practitioner in a young child's learning and development and highlights the early educational value of good quality adult-child interactions. This is supported by the REPEY study, which found effective early years pedagogy involved practitioners engaging with children in a process of "cognitive construction" by using open questioning to extend their thinking (Siraj-Blatchford et al, 2002a, p.3). These studies found that "positive cognitive outcomes are closely associated with adult-child interactions … that involve some element of sustained shared thinking" (Siraj-Blatchford and Sylva, 2004, p.720). Sustained shared thinking is the means by which practitioners nurture and develop critical thinking skills within children. It involves seeking out opportunities to build upon the children's interests and challenging them to indulge in a deeper thought process. It is best defined in the EPPE report:

> 'Sustained shared thinking' occurs when two or more individuals 'work together' in an intellectual way to solve a problem, clarify a concept, evaluate an activity, extend a narrative etc. Both parties must contribute to the thinking and it must develop and extend the understanding. (Siraj-Blatchford et al, 2004, p.vi)

Dowling explains that sustained shared thinking can occur when children share their thinking with adults as well as when they converse with one another in

---

Children need access to continuous provision with time and space to become involved in what interests them	Projects follow the lead of the children. This means that practitioners seeking to engage with children will be doing so on the children's terms, making it more likely that the interactions will be sustained
Practitioners need to have an appreciation of cultural difference and welcome thinking that builds upon personal experience	When involve in project work, children are encouraged to draw from their own individual spheres of experience and share these in order to further each other's thinking
Children should be given plenty of opportunities to practice and apply skills	Projects provide a wealth of opportunities for practitioners to help children develop a range of critical thinking skills. Following are several examples of this in relation to the where is George? provocation
Children should be able to see and reflect upon their learning in written and pictorial records	The culminating learning story or display produced during a project makes this possible and provides practitioners with a visual stimulus for encouraging reflective thought

Diagram 1: Conditions which promote sustained shared thinking (Dowling M, 2005, p. 10)

small groups. She sets out "appropriate contexts" for developing sustained shared thinking (2005, p.10). These should be considered in relation to the project approach in order to illustrate how projects provide practitioners with opportunities to extend children's thought processes. Diagram 1 on page 35 outlines the conditions Dowling suggests are needed for promoting sustained shared thinking and explains how project work provides for these.

Developing creative and critical thinking skills

Critical thinking skills must be introduced early in order for children to develop as learners and thrive in the future. Promoting sustained shared thinking prepares young children for their futures as life-long learners. Children who have such transferable life skills as the ability to enquire, consider, reflect, reason, predict, evaluate and solve, will be better equipped to succeed in a world where a job is no longer for life and careers are constantly evolving. Creative thinking skills are

important because they help people to adapt and take a flexible approach when faced with difficult or unusual situations. Creative thinkers are more able to "take risks, think flexibly, be innovative, play with ideas and respond imaginatively" (Duffy, 2010, p.20).

Revisions of British early years curriculum in recent years have given prominence to creative and critical thinking skills. The EYFS draws upon the recommendations of KEEP (DfES, 2005), highlighting the importance of valuing and modeling creativity as well as challenging and extending children's thinking (DCSF, 2007, Principles into Practice Card 4.3). The Welsh Foundation Phase Framework underlines the fundamental importance of developing "thinking across the curriculum" to enable children to think creatively and critically" (DCELLS, 2008a, p.10). The Northern Ireland Curriculum specifically places emphasis upon "the explicit development of Thinking Skills and Personal Capabilities" (CCEA, 2007, p.2) and provides a guiding framework for this purpose. Furthermore, Scotland's Curriculum for Excellence guidance for early years practitioners promotes "active learning" because it "engages and challenges children's thinking" (Scottish Executive, 2007, p.5).

A creative and critical thinker is someone who is able to apply knowledge to a variety of situations; able to process and analyse a range of information; has the ability to consider a problem and look for possible solutions; and has the foresight to pre-empt likely obstacles and creatively plan around these. In order to learn critical thinking skills children must be given the opportunity to immerse themselves in a deeper thought process with the help of skilled practitioners: "With the right stimulus and support all children can learn to think in ways that enable them to solve problems, be inventive and make discoveries..." (Bayley and Broadbent, 2002, p.i).

Dowling describes "types of thinking" and makes suggestions for how practitioners might sustain them (2005, p.10). In addition, Clarke (2007) offers a comprehensive overview of the different thinking skills and explains why they are so important for young children at the beginning of their journey towards becoming independent and competent thinkers. Both of these are used as a basis for the following examples taken from the where is George? provocation to demonstrate how the project approach fosters children's creative and critical thinking skills.

A note about friendship

As Katz and Chard (2000) point out, it is important to encourage young children to mix and build relationships with different peers. However, care should be taken when dividing children into pairs or groups in order to undertake project tasks. Young children need to feel safe and secure in the knowledge that they will not be placed under undue pressure or put into awkward or difficult situations.

Children who are anxious or unhappy will find it difficult to fully engage with the others in their group. This will stifle their enthusiasm and impact upon their ability to concentrate on the task in hand, ultimately having a detrimental affect upon their learning (Isaacs S, 1930). Practitioners should bear this in mind before splitting up friendship groups (Broadhead P, 2004). The social and collaborative process of project work is most successful when children learn from each other. Therefore, there is no need to divide children up according to ability.

Learning how to process information

In the example on page 38 the children recognised the bench as one that is similar to those they have seen in the parks they play in. Making this connection led them to realise that George might be in a park. The practitioner then helped extend the children's thought process by asking them to consider why George might be in a park. This encouraged the children to reason and provide explanations for their ideas.

Information processing skills

Information-processing skills enable children to investigate and explore, and gather and use information (Dowling, 2005). As Clarke explains, these skills enable children to "see links between different pieces of information" and helps them to decide which information is most valuable and worth retaining (2007, p.11).

The example above shows how young children can be helped to gather and process information on a basic level. The children decided which information was important in the case of their missing friend; they collated this information and displayed it in order to reflect upon it. The role-play scenario provided an age-appropriate playful context within which to do this.

Reasoning skills

Reasoning skills enable children to use logic; make connections; give reasons for opinions and explain actions; and make informed judgements and decisions. Clarke (2007) highlights the importance of language development and communication skills in this respect.

Enquiry skills

Enquiry skills enable children to ask relevant questions; plan what to do; and speculate upon and predict outcomes. Although young children are naturally inquisitive they often have difficulty formulating questions in order to gather the information they require (Clarke, 2007). Charlesworth (2005) suggests that children should be encouraged to ask questions in order to develop their enquiry skills, but they first need to understand what questions are and how they are formed. This is something that practitioners should model often and children should have plenty of practice doing: "The notion of a question, what it is, how it is formulated and how it can help further their learning all need to be made explicit to children" (Charlesworth, 2005, p.117).

As previously mentioned, the children in this class speak English as an additional language making it difficult for some to clearly express themselves to others. It follows that, for these children, formulating questions is more difficult than for children who already have a confident grasp of the language.

In the example on page 39 the practitioner understood the needs of these children and provided guidance in order to ensure that they would be fully prepared to carry out their investigations. Her scaffolding enabled them to formulate questions and compile a description.

Creative thinking and problem solving skills

Creative thinking and problem solving skills enable children to come up with ideas and suggestions and use their imagination to think of creative solutions. Clarke (2007) draws attention to the need for children to be open to suggestion and not afraid of making mistakes. Creative thinkers have the ability to accept failure and think of an alternative plan.

The example on page 39 demonstrates creative thinking in young children on a basic level. These children cannot prove that George is in Manningham Park simply because he is sitting at a picnic bench in what looks like a park. Furthermore, even if they are right about this they are concerned that he might not be safe there on his own. Their solution to this problem is to go and see if they can find him and bring him back home.

Evaluation skills

Evaluation skills enable children to reflect, recall and evaluate information in order to formulate opinions.

The children in the examples on page 40 are recalling events from the past two weeks and reflecting upon them with their puppet George. This is the beginning stage in their progress towards developing evaluation skills. Although seemingly insignificant, these conversations with George are the laying foundations for later educational challenges that involve the further step of evaluating information. Learning stories and displays are particularly useful for helping children to evaluate information and an example of this is provided in the second part of this book.

Fostering creative and imaginative thought

The introduction of the National Curriculum in 1988 and the subsequent implementation of the Primary Strategies in the late nineties resulted in an

Developing reasoning skills: an example

An anonymous person sent in a photograph of George sitting at a picnic bench. The children were gathered on the carpet and shown the picture:

Ms Matthews: Where about is he?
Aliyah: On the bench.
Zeleha: He's sleeping.
Ms Matthews: He's sleeping on the bench. Where do you think the bench is?

Several children started shouting at once. Some stood up and ran to the front.

Ms Matthews: You've got to use your language and tell me. He's on the bench. Where do you think the bench is?
Isa: Over there!
Ms Matthews: That's a picture!
Khalisah: In the park.
Ms Matthews: What kind of park?
Khalisah: Manningham.
Aliyah: And we've got a different park. There's a new one.
Ms Matthews: Which park do you think George is in?
Aliyah: Manningham.
Ms Matthews: How do you know it's a park?
Aqsa: I know. I go there.
Ms Matthews: And what do you see when you go to the park?
Isa: Ducks.
Abu-Bakr: Trees.
Sunehri: And slides.
Ms Matthews: If there are other ducks at the park, why do you think George has gone to the park?
Isa: To play with them.
Ms Matthews: Yeah maybe. That could be it.
Isa: He's a duck. That's why the other ducks came to him.

increased academic emphasis in primary schools (Broadhead, 2004; Anning, 2005). This impacted upon foundation stage provision and had a detrimental effect upon the creative approaches to teaching and learning (Bayley and Broadbent, 2002).

Developing enquiry skills: an example

When the class decided to interview other children and members of staff from around the school, Ms. Matthew's knew that they would need some time to prepare and so divided them into talk partners and asked them to think of some questions. The initial suggestions were as follows:

Zeleha: We lost the George! There nowhere. He lost. We not find him.
Raheem: George has gone home and he's not in the classroom.
Hamzah: George gone!

Although the children were able to convey their problem with the use of statements, they demonstrated a lack of understanding about what a question was. Ms. Matthews provided the children with some example questions, i.e. "have you seen George?", "do you think George might have gone out somewhere?" and "where is George?". She then prompted the children by starting them off with some question stems, i.e. "have you...", "do you..." and "where..." which some children were able to complete:

Isa: Have you seen George in the dinner hall?
Aishah: Do you think George is outside?
Haroon: Where is George anyway?
Aishah: What's happened to George?

Ms. Matthews explained that it was all very well asking people where George is but they might not know what he looks like. The children needed to put together a description. Ms. Matthews acted as a scribe for the children as they described his appearance:

Khalisah: He's fluffy. He's got fluffy hair everywhere. He's got feet.
Aliyah: ...and wings.
Khalisah: ...orange mouth.
Isa: ...black eyes.

This preparation helped the children a great deal.

Developing creative thinking and problem solving skills: an example

After much discussion about where George might be in the photograph, the children became a little concerned for his safety.

Ms Matthews: Do you think we know where he is now?
Khalisah: I think we have to go there.
Ms Matthews: Why?
Khalisah: Because then he's gonna get lost. People are gonna take him.
Haroon: Yeah. Another duck will eat him! No a Tiger will eat him. Tigers are strong.
Khalisah: We have to bring him back to the school.
Ms Matthews: I think that's a really good idea. I think I could take a group of children this afternoon and we'll go and have a look for him.

This conversation led to a visit to the park to find George.

Learning how to recall and reflect upon events

Developing evaluation skills: an example

After two weeks George returned and the children were eager to tell him about the past two weeks' events:

Khalisah: We missed you!
Zeleha: We was finding him. We sawed the bench and you wasn't there.
Aisha: We got a picture of him. It's over there.
Haroon: He was on the computer picture.

Aisha took George to look at the picture of him sitting at the picnic table in the park.

There is a growing movement in support of bringing creativity back into early education (Open EYE, 2010; Tims, 2010) and the child-centred ideology represented in current British early years curricular places renewed emphasis on the provision of a creative curriculum that starts with the child.

Dowling includes "fantasizing" and "imagining" in her list of thinking skills (2005, p.10). In order to fully participate and enjoy the where is George? provocation the children were required to suspend their disbelief and think imaginatively. According to Rattigan (2008) young children need such opportunities in order to develop their lateral thinking skills and personal creativity. Clarke further explains that creative thinking "enables the learner to look for alternatives, not always accepting the first answer" (2007, p.12). In order to help children achieve this higher level of cognition it is important to provide an environment where imaginative thought is welcomed and children are confident to express their own opinions (Charlesworth, 2005). They should be exposed to open-ended experiences and encouraged to offer ideas without fear of failure. The provocation format is an ideal medium through which to encourage creative thought.

Asking the right questions

Wood places emphasis upon the use of effective questioning in promoting thinking skills. He explains that questions should be structured so as to

encourage children to develop their thinking and "to reason, to hypothesize and to generate their own theories" (1998, cited in Moyles et al, 2002). Thornton and Brunton (2004) point out that promoting such skills is not easy and explain the difficulties practitioners face in "judging the appropriate intervention". They suggest that practitioners "need to maintain sensitivity to individual children's needs for support, while knowing how to intervene in a way that does not inhibit their thoughts and actions". This involves the practitioner carefully listening and observing in order to seek out opportunities to build upon the children's interests and challenge them to indulge in a deeper thought process. Projects provide an ideal arena in which to do this. Children are engaged in investigations that perpetuate their interests and absorb them in ongoing open-ended activities. This gives practitioners ample opportunity to become involved in the children's thought processes by introducing lines of questioning and enquiry. Some practical ideas for helping practitioners use open questioning can be found on page 62.

The where is George? provocation is an example of how project work helps children to develop communications skills by fostering social interaction between children and adults. Furthermore, project work provides practitioners with opportunities to promote sustained shared thinking, helping children to develop the creative and critical thinking skills they need to become life-long learners.

Key points

- **Project work supports the view that children learn through interaction with others.**

- **The project approach promotes social interaction, which helps children develop their communication skills and improves their learning chances.**

- **The social interaction involved in project work creates opportunities for practitioners to engage children in sustained shared thinking. This helps children to develop a range of creative and critical thinking skills that are needed for successful life-long learning.**

Part Two: The project approach in action

So far this book has provided some examples of simple open-ended provocations that were set up and allowed to evolve organically without any set structure or format. This second part of the book takes a practical look at carrying out a full-scale planned project. It offers:

■ Suggestions for finding starting points

■ Details of the planning process with explanatory examples of how to create planning documents

■ A consideration of the central importance of collecting, interpreting and documenting observations

■ Explanations of how this documentation is used to inform the development of a project

■ Links throughout to adaptable and printable planning and observation documents, which are contained on a separate CD-Rom attached to the inside front cover of the book

A cyclical process

Project work is a cyclical process involving open-ended planning that is informed by ongoing observation, reflection, discussion and interpretation (see Figure 2). Throughout the life of a project, practitioners observe the children's activities, investigations and conversation. They then take time to reflect upon their observations before sharing and discussing them with each other, as well as the children. Practitioners meet regularly throughout the life of a project to review this documentation and develop planning in response. This ongoing observation and interpretation is referred to by Rinaldi as a "spiral of documentation" (2000, quoted in Thornton and Brunton, 2009, p.110) and is used to inform the continuing development of the project.

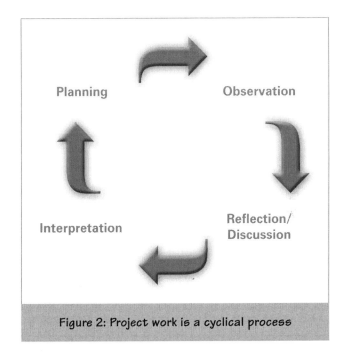

Figure 2: Project work is a cyclical process

The following explanation about planning, carrying out and documenting project work is very much influenced by the underlying child-centred principles represented by the Reggio approach in combination with the more structured framework provided by Katz and Chard (1989; 2000).

Identifying an interest

A project is most likely to grab the attention of the children if it stems from their own particular interests and fascinations. There are various ways of picking out a starting point for a project, which could be triggered by any number of things. An idea may come as a direct result of a child's actions or questions. On the other hand, practitioners might build upon observed interests and use them as inspiration for setting up a provocation. For example:

A topic: The children might be interested in a particular aspect of a current topic. For example, those learning about outer space might be curious about the kind of food astronauts eat, which may lead to an investigation into dried foods.

An object: A child may bring something into the setting. This might be a religious artifact, leading to a project about a particular religious festival. Or it might be a holiday souvenir from another country, leading to an exploration of the customs of the people from another culture. Otherwise, the practitioner might recognise that the children have a particular interest in something and introduce or plant an object somewhere in the setting that

triggers an investigation. The cocoon provocation on page 10 is an example of this.

An event: This could include birthdays, festivals, holidays, parties, births, deaths, visits and visitors, or doctor, dentist and optician appointments. The excitement, anticipation, concern or anxiety surrounding any of these is reason to delve into an exploration that leads to gaining deeper knowledge and understanding.

A question: A child might ask a question that offers a perfect opportunity for a large-scale in depth investigation. Otherwise, the children might have

All about eggs

Horton Grange Primary School, Bradford

This project was carried out in an 80-place nursery in an inner city community primary school in Bradford, where the majority of children speak English as an additional language. The project emerged from the nursery's topic about farming and was planned in response to a provoking farm visit. While at the farm the children experienced holding a young chick on their arm and were amazed when the farmer brought out a full-grown chicken and demonstrated how chickens lay eggs.

The following day the children were brought together in their home groups to talk about the visit. The children remembered feeding the animals, climbing on a tractor, seeing mother animals with their babies, and then washing their hands to prevent the spread of germs. However, the predominant and reoccurring theme was chickens and eggs and the children were particularly excited when recalling the chicken laying the egg, describing it as a magic trick. It seemed that this interest in eggs was also due in part to the upcoming Easter festival and the school Easter Egg Competition, which had been launched the previous week.

A project called 'all about eggs' was launched and during the weeks that followed the children: investigated what happens when eggs are broken; learned about different methods of cooking eggs;

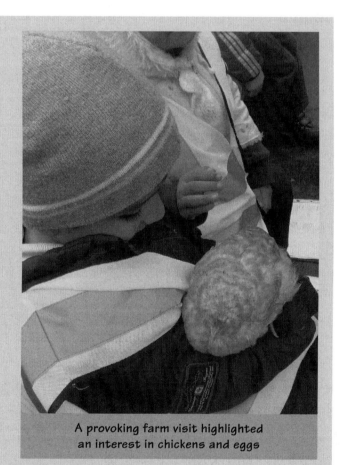

A provoking farm visit highlighted an interest in chickens and eggs

examined and compared the properties of raw and cooked egg; looked closely at a variety of eggs produced by different farm birds; and learned a little about the journey of the egg from farm to shop. In response to the children's high level of interest, the practitioners also hired an incubator from a local farm and during the following term the children were treated to the real-life spectacle of chicken eggs hatching.

Deciding which interests to follow

Issues and concerns

Practitioners are faced with the difficult decision about which of the children's interests to use as the inspiration for a project. There is an issue here about whether it is a good idea to plan a whole group project based upon the specific interests of just one child, or whether to look for a common interest that seems to be shared by a majority of the children in the group.

Of course it is impossible to find an interest that is guaranteed to be shared by every single child in a group, especially in larger settings. This is the case whether planning a theme or a project. Not everyone is going to share the same interests. Although it is not possible to plan a single project that caters to the interests of all, it is possible to plan a series of projects that aim to follow the interests of different children in turn. This can be done proportionately; for instance, a project planned to build upon the interests of the majority of children in a group would be large-scale and planned to last a number of weeks. However, a project planned to build on the interests of fewer children would be smaller and last just a couple of days to a week. It is also possible, but logistically complicated, to plan small-scale projects for individuals to undertake in their own time.

When involving children in a project that might not specifically cater to their interests, it is possible to enthuse them by looking for angles that might capture their imagination. For example, a child might not be particularly interested in a project about paramedics and ambulances, but may be interested in fast vehicles. A practitioner could create a link here and encourage the child to find out what type of vehicle would make a good ambulance. Furthermore, it is also a good idea to involve less interested children by giving them tasks that suit their particular aptitudes and abilities. For example, although a child might not be interested in how a bicycle wheel turns, they might be exceptionally good at drawing. A practitioner can use this talent to encourage the child's involvement by asking her to draw a picture of the bike wheel mechanisms.

been observed while deeply involved in certain play activities. For example, they may have been burying various objects in the sandpit, leading a practitioner to ask such questions as, "how can you make it easier to find what you have buried?" or "how can you make sure no one finds what you've buried?"

A picture: The children might be preoccupied with a particular current news event and a practitioner may come across an interesting photograph on a news website and use this as a trigger for discussion; or the children may be observed practising and experimenting with a particular creative technique and a practitioner might display a print of a related artwork in the art area in response; or an incident relating to personal safety, friendship or routine might occur in the setting, leading a practitioner to take a photo of some puppets in precarious situations as a trigger for conversation and debate (Bayley, 2006).

Children's specific interests: These may be more obvious for those practitioners who work with small numbers of children and have the opportunity to enter into in-depth discussion on a regular basis. For practitioners working in larger settings it will be necessary to reflect upon observation records to identify the children's specific interests as they come to light through playful activity. Cross-referencing these records will also help to determine where children share the same interests and preoccupations in different areas. For example, there might be some children who frequently enjoy role-play involving paramedics and hospitals. A project about the emergency health services could be planned in response to this. Otherwise, a group of children may repeatedly return to washing the cars and bikes outside, leading to a project about the car wash. There may also be individual children who, separately at various times, show an ongoing interest in building towers using various building materials. This could lead to a project investigating the best way to build a strong, tall tower. Inspiration for a project might also come from a favourite story or nursery rhyme.

Finding out what the children already know

Once an area of interest has been identified the children are then gathered together for a further discussion or mind-mapping session so that practitioners can gain a clearer idea about their understanding of the topic and if there are any areas where they have difficulties.

The mind-mapping session for the all about eggs project revealed that, despite visiting the farm, the children were unsure about where eggs come from and how they come to be available for sale in shops. There was also some confusion about why chicks hatch out of some eggs but not others. Most of the children, however, had some experience of seeing eggs being cooked at home and had a good level of knowledge and understanding in this area, apart from being able to explain how eggs are boiled.

A mind-mapping session

Finding out what the children would like to learn

As well as finding out what the children already know about a subject, it is also important to find out which aspects of the subject the children are most fascinated with. This helps to ensure that the project is developed in line with the children's interests, which motivates them to want to learn and find out more. Practitioners can identify such interests within their observations of the children's reactions to the initial provocation and their play in the days following. A planned focused activity about the subject will reveal more still.

In the case of the all about eggs project, while observing the children examining the eggs in the investigation area, it became apparent that the children were quite hesitant and unsure about cracking them open. One little girl was observed accidentally dropping an egg on the floor. Looking around nervously, she hid her hands under the table. Once reassured that it was all right, she smiled, picked up the egg and began to bash it on the table until it broke completely. She then spent a long while mixing the raw egg with her fingers before rubbing it around a plate with her hands. Another child was keen to show practitioners a

Humpty Dumpty he had created by cutting out an egg shape and sticking strips of paper to it as limbs. A conversation with the boy revealed that he had difficulty explaining why eggs break when they fall.

An initial introductory activity about eggs was also set up. This was done for two reasons. As well as helping practitioners to find out what the children were most interested in, the activity provided an opportunity for the children to closely examine and talk about eggs with an adult, which was especially important in light of their need for support in English language development. During the activity the children looked closely at a variety of different farm eggs. They matched the eggs to photos of birds and examined them more closely with magnifiers. The eggs were cracked open, yolks compared in size and colour, and the children were invited to touch raw egg and describe how it felt. However, the most interesting and revealing aspect of the activity was when the children inevitably dropped some eggs on the floor by accident. Each time this happened the responsible children looked a little surprised and worried. Once reassured however, there was a lot of excitement with children gathering around and competing to scoop up the egg and crack the shell open.

Using mind maps when planning a project: an example

A mind map is used to inform planning so that the project will:

- Fill any gaps in the children's knowledge;

- Answer any questions the children might have;

- Build on the specific interests of the children.

In the case of the all about eggs project, the children were gathered together for a mind-mapping session about eggs. This enabled practitioners to get a better grasp on the children's existing knowledge about chickens and eggs and highlight those areas where the children were less sure.

When mind mapping with younger children, it is a good idea to divide them into smaller groups. This makes the process more manageable for the practitioner, but also more beneficial to the children because each will have more time and opportunity to speak. In this case the children were divided into their home groups (groups of 10).

Younger children, or those with special educational needs will benefit from the use of picture cues. The all about eggs project was carried out with three and four-year-old children, of which a large proportion speak English as an additional language. As a result practitioners ensured that they used photographs from the farm visit as well as pictures of farm birds and eggs as cues to prompt discussion.

When creating a mind map it is useful to compile a list of questions that the practitioner can use to draw information out of the children. Some of the questions used in this case were:

- What is an egg?

- Where do eggs come from?

- Where did Farmer James get the egg from?

- What did the egg at the farm feel like?

- What can you do with eggs?

- Have you ever eaten an egg?

- How do you like your eggs cooked?

Many of these questions asked the children to draw on their memories of the farm visit, as well as their home experiences. This made it easier for the children to think of responses.

A mind map might simply be a list of questions with the children's responses written underneath. Otherwise it might look like a web, featuring the subject matter at the centre with practitioner questions branching off. Figure 3 on page 46 shows the mind-map created for the all about eggs project.

Key Points

- **Project work is a cyclical process involving open-ended planning that is informed by ongoing observation, reflection, discussion and interpretation.**

- **A project is started with an initial provocation, for example, a topic, object, event, question, picture or specific interest identified in children's play.**

- **Children are involved in mind-mapping exercises and the information gained is used to plan the focus of the project.**

Open-ended planning

Once the children's interests have been identified, practitioners meet to discuss their observations, decide upon some starting points for further investigation and create some initial planning documents. Projects are open-ended and developed through a process of ongoing observation and discussion, evolving in line with the children's interests and needs. This means that much of the planning is retrospective, outlining some starter activities with predicted outcomes but leaving space for practitioners to fill in additional activities and outcomes as they transpire. The flexibility of this planning enables practitioners to be dynamic in their approach, observing and formatively assessing their activities as they progress and responding to the children's changing intentions. Practitioners regularly reflect upon the children's activities throughout a project and highlight curriculum learning objectives accordingly. This is instead of a plan that asks the practitioner to steer the children in a particular direction to meet predetermined objectives. **Planning in this way supports the role of the practitioner as a guide rather than a leader.**

The planning produced for a project will depend upon the type and size of setting, available resources and number of practitioners. The planning for the nursery at Horton Grange is intricate and detailed and caters for a large number of children with wide ranging needs. Furthermore, the nursery is bound by whole school targets put in place as part of an ongoing effort to continually improve since the school was recently released from special measures. These whole

school targets are writing, reading and mathematical calculation. General targets relating to these areas are chosen as a focus in the nursery each half term and activities are planned with these in mind. The all about eggs project aims to demonstrate how a project can be planned while taking account of existing routines and curriculum commitments.

Adult-led focused activities

When carrying out a project with younger children it is useful to plan some adult-led focused activities that aim to develop their knowledge and understanding of the subject area. The children can then draw on this when involved in later investigations and child-initiated activities. Figure 4 on page 48 shows the planning created for focused activities at the beginning of the all about eggs project, addressing the main areas where the children had gaps in their knowledge about

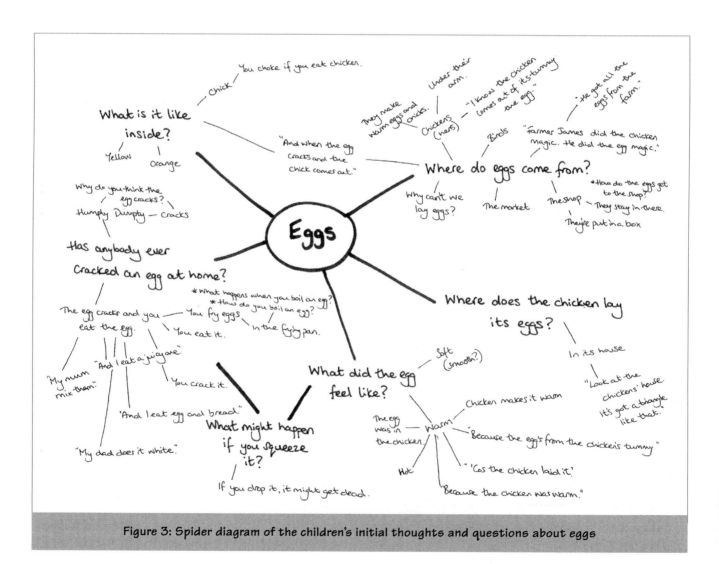

Figure 3: Spider diagram of the children's initial thoughts and questions about eggs

eggs. Practitioners planned these activities around the question: where do eggs come from? The activities aimed to improve the children's understanding about the production and distribution of eggs, as well as build their vocabulary and further their English language development. The initial introductory activity about eggs is also included on this plan. The plan includes a section for practitioners to retrospectively record any interesting observations that might have implications for future planning. It also provides space for adding ideas for other focused activities that emerge as the project progresses.

Adult-supported group investigation

Educators in Reggio Emilia place particular emphasis upon group learning experiences where adults and children work together to construct knowledge and understanding. It is through group work that children find out about the benefits of being exposed to a variety of perspectives (Thornton and Brunton, 2009), and with adult support, they learn how to listen to each other, express ideas and work cooperatively together (Thornton and Brunton, 2007). It is not just the children who learn through group investigation. Practitioners also benefit from being part of the group and being directly involved in the discussion and debate, which enables them to gain a deeper insight into the children's learning. The number of children as well as the number of staff available will dictate how many focused group investigations are planned to run at any one time. The age and ability of the children will also determine how complex any particular investigation is and to what extent the children are able to take the lead.

The nursery in this example has a number of curriculum commitments including regular phonics input and literacy, numeracy and personal, social and emotional focus activities, as well as daily structured story time and singing sessions. It was therefore decided that these should run as usual and the all about eggs project be planned to run alongside them. As a result, just one adult-supported group investigation was planned and carried out during free-flow activity time. The investigation was planned to address one particular question that seemed to be of most interest to the children: Why and how do eggs crack? The planning document created for this investigation is shown in Figure 5 on page 50.

Setting up an initial focused activity can help to identify predominant interests

Trusting that children will participate at an appropriate level

Issues and concerns

Allowing the children to take part on their own terms and at their own level may concern practitioners because of the risk that some children might not challenge themselves sufficiently and realise their full potential, or conversely, take on too difficult a challenge with little chance of success.

The ongoing communication involved in project work allows practitioners to continually assess whether individual children are on task and participating at an appropriate level. Well considered open- questioning enables practitioners to help children develop their ideas and reach a higher level of thought. Careful questioning can also be used to guide children and help them reflect upon and assess how they are doing with a particular task. Observation is key because it enables practitioners to target support and plan to meet individual needs.

Nursery – Ms Matthews/Miss Cahill Spring B – Project – All About Eggs – Adult-led focused activities

Activity	EYFS Areas of Learning and Development	Key Questions	Key Vocabulary	Observations: Implications for Future Planning
Initial introductory activity – eggs Show children a selection of eggs. Compare and talk about eggshells. Crack eggs open and compare size and colour of yolks. Encourage children to touch raw egg and talk about how it feels.	Investigate a variety of eggs using sight, touch and smell (KUW). Look closely at similarities and differences in eggs (KUW). Speak clearly and audibly with confidence when talking about eggs (CLL). Extend vocabulary, exploring the meanings and sounds of new words (CLL).	Where do eggs come from? What can you tell me about the colour of the shells? What is the difference about that yolk? How does the raw egg feel? Do you know how to crack an egg open?	Egg, chicken, duck, quail, goose, rhea, turkey, hen, eggshell, pattern, colour, yolk, egg white, raw, cold, warm, slimy, sticky, yellow, orange.	Children very interested in eggshell – scrunching it with fingers and breaking it apart. Put some eggshell in the collage area and empty shells in the investigation area. Children excited by accidental breaking of eggs when dropped. Also seemed a bit worried. Investigation – breaking eggs.
The journey of the egg from farm to shop Watch video on Espresso 'With the Hens'. Use sequencing cards show how eggs are produced at a farm, collected, packed and transported to the supermarket.	Find out about where eggs come from and how they come to be available in shops (KUW).	Where do eggs come from? Where can you buy eggs? How do you think eggs are transported from the farm to the shop?	Eggs, chicken, roost, farm, egg box, collect, pack, lorry, transport, shop, market, supermarket.	Provide books and pictures of creatures that are similar in colour or have legs/antennae of the same shape to help children with investigations. Help children to find out which creatures create cocoons. Leave creature in cocoon and discuss this further tomorrow morning. Ensure plenty of opportunity at the beginning of next week to continue this.
The Egg Read The Egg. Find out about how information can be found in non-fiction texts (CLL).	Show and understand about how information can be found in non-fiction texts (CLL). Find out about eggs and what needs to happen for them to develop into chicks (KUW).	What comes out of the egg? How does the chicken look after the egg? Where do eggs come from?	Egg, chicken, chick, nesting box, warm, incubate, hatch.	Children very interested in why some eggs hatch and others do not. Put some nesting boxes and pretend eggs in the farm role-play. Incubate chicken eggs.
Cooking eggs Cook eggs in a variety of ways. Fried, scrambled, omelette, boiled. Involved children in preparation. Encourage them to talk about changes as they happen to eggs during preparation and cooking.	Use talk to organise, sequence and clarify thinking and ideas about how to cook eggs (CLL). Find out about the different ways of cooking eggs (KUW). Investigate eggs using sight, touch, smell and taste (KUW).	How do you like to eat your eggs? How do you scramble/fry/boil and egg? What is happening to the egg?	Egg, boil, water, fry, oil, scrambled, mix, cook, heat, hot, bread, toast, white, yellow, yolk.	Children unsure about boiling eggs. Take photos of different cooking methods and put in home corner with cooking utensils, egg boxes and toy eggs.

Figure 4: Planning for adult-led focused activities for the all about eggs project

ADAPTABLE RESOURCE

A focused activity to find out what
happens when eggs are cooked

Both children and adults benefit
from group investigations

Planning to enhance continuous provision

Gandini of Reggio Children refers to the learning environment as "the third educator" and emphasises the importance of continually developing it with careful planning (1998, p.177). For many early years settings it is usual practice to enhance the learning environment with topic-related activities and resources. Often this involves creating a topic-web of subject-based ideas borne out of the practitioners' own imaginations. Although this is a good way of ensuring the children are experiencing a range of activities and meeting specific curriculum goals, planning in this way will not necessarily capture the imaginations of the children. Like all other aspects of project planning, the learning environment plans represent a balance of adult and child-initiated activities, and are open-ended so that they can be developed in line with the children's interests. Thornton and Brunton offer some useful advice with respect to this. They suggest that practitioners plan some activities that meet specific learning intentions but reserve space in the planning for "emergent objectives" (2007, p.76).

The setting in this example produces overview classroom enhancement plans for both the indoor and outside areas. These are related to the current topic and detail additional activities and resources to be provided alongside the usual continuous provision available to the children when they are involved in free-flow activity time. After some consideration the planning documents were redesigned to enable practitioners to take a more open-ended approach and allow space to plan in line with the interests and needs of the children as they emerged during the project.

Figure 6 on page 52 is an abridged example of the planning documents used for enhancing the learning environment. With whole school targets in mind, it was decided that a small number of farm topic activities should remain (labelled as adult-initiated). In addition, it was decided that a number of farm themed toys and resources should continue to be easily accessible to the children. However, much of the documents were left blank and additional enhancements were planned as the project progressed. At the end of the project the practitioners cross-referenced the activities with the EYFS to identify where curriculum goals and whole-school targets had been met. This demonstrates how

Nursery – Ms Matthews/Miss Cahill Spring B – Project – All About Eggs – Adult-supported group investigation

Investigation: Breaking eggs

Ask children about their experiences of breaking eggs. Ask them for suggestions about how to break eggs. Allow children to try breaking eggs in various ways. Encourage children to touch and describe the feel of raw egg.

EYFS Areas of Learning and Development	Key questions	Key vocabulary
Investigate eggs by using sight, touch, smell, and hearing (KUW).	What might happen if I throw this egg on the floor?	Egg, break, smash, shell, crack, yolk, slimy, sticky, runny, cold, wet, broken, sharp, yellow, mix.
Extend their vocabulary, exploring the meaning and sounds of new words (CLL).	Have you ever dropped an egg? Tell me about it.	
	What do you think will come out?	
Use talk to organise, sequence and clarify thinking and ideas about how to break eggs (CLL).	What did it sound like?	
	How would you like to break the egg?	
Move with control and coordination when breaking the eggs (PD).	What does the raw egg/shell feel like?	
	What has happened to the egg?	

Additional curriculum learning

Be confident to break eggs and make a mess (PSED).

Be confident to touch raw egg (PSED).

Manage personal hygiene – wash hands after handling eggs (PSED).

Observations: implications for future planning

Some children unsure about breaking the egg – hesitant. Most wanted to crack the egg carefully against a surface with hands.

Fill empty eggshells with paint and throw at large paper.

Most children keen to feel the raw egg. Some very reluctant.

Make slime for malleable area to encourage this type of sensory experience.

One child tried to bounce the egg. Unsure about concept.

Experiment with objects made out of various materials to see if they bounce.

Some children tried to taste the raw egg or put fingers in mouths.

Talk about washing hands and consequences of eating raw egg.

Figure 5: Open-ended planning for the adult-supported group investigation from the all about eggs project.

ADAPTABLE RESOURCE

it is possible to meet curriculum expectations in the context of project work while still following the lead of the children to a large extent.

As explained in the first part of this book, projects can be planned with varying degrees of complexity. **The above planning examples were used for a full-scale planned project. However, the planning for a simple provocation that does not have a set structure or format will look quite different. In this case the planning is fully retrospective, outlining predicted outcomes but leaving space for practitioners to fill in actual outcomes as they transpire.** The planning documents for each of the provocations featured in the first part of this book are included on the CD-Rom and provide examples of the various ways that such plans might be produced.

Key Points

- **Planning for a full-scale project involves:**

  - **Planning adult-led focused activities that aim to develop children's knowledge and understanding of the subject area;**

  - **Planning adult-supported group investigations that aim to provide an opportunity for children and adults to work together and gain new knowledge through group exploration and discussion;**

  - **Providing resources and guidance for children who choose to undertake their own independent investigations and activities.**

- **The planning for a simple provocation is fully retrospective, outlining predicted outcomes but leaving space for practitioners to fill in actual outcomes as they transpire.**

The role of the practitioner

During a project practitioners have three main tasks: (1) listening to the children and documenting their learning; (2) reflecting upon, discussing and interpreting this documentation to inform ongoing planning and; (3) providing resources and intellectual guidance during investigative work. This section outlines how these tasks are carried out with some practical examples to illustrate.

A lack of structure and control

Issues and concerns

The thought of open-ended planning may be of concern because of a perceived lack of structure and control. Some practitioners may prefer a more systematic method of curriculum coverage and a more direct approach to delivery.

The planning examples for the provocations and project featured in this book demonstrate that it is possible to highlight curriculum coverage retrospectively and keep a clear record of this. Practitioners who prefer to keep systematic records can produce an overview of curriculum areas of learning and development and highlight and date areas covered over a period of time. Practitioners can then plan to address any areas that are missed using different methods.

Examining raw egg in the investigation area

Nursery Environment Enhancement Plan – Spring B – Project – All About Eggs

Targets: Reading – I can talk about the pictures in the book.
Writing – I can hold a pencil correctly. Numeracy – I can touch count

Area of Provision	Children's Interests	Enhancements
Reading	Adult-initiated	**Adult role:** Encourage the children to talk about the picture in the books and share their experiences of the visit. **Enhancement:** Photo books from farm visit. **T:** I can talk about the pictures in a book.
Storytelling	Adult-initiated	**Adult role:** Share and retell The Odd Egg. **Enhancement:** Pictures of birds and eggs from in the book. **T:** I can talk about the pictures in a book.
Writing		
KUW (investigation area)	Adult-initiated	**Adult role:** Question the children about what they can see, feel and smell. Encourage use of key vocabulary. **Enhancement:** Variety of raw and cooked eggs, eggshells and magnifiers.
Themed role play	Interest in how some eggs hatch as chicks and others do not	**Adult role:** Talk about how chickens nest an incubate their eggs to keep them warm. **Enhancement:** Cardboard boxes, toy chickens, straw and pretend eggs.
Maths area		
Music		
Small world	Adult-initiated	**Adult role:** Encourage the children to talk about the animals that they have seen on the farm. **Enhancement:** Small world farm.
Home corner	Transferral of eggshell to role-play. Interest in cooking and eating eggs. Lack of understanding about boiling eggs.	**Adult role:** Refer to the photos and talk about different ways that eggs can be prepared. Talk about how eggs are used in various recipes. **Enhancement:** Photos of eggs cooking, frying pan, saucepan, whisk, spatulas, egg boxes, pretend eggs.
Collage	Enjoyment at crushing eggshell. Interest in how it felt.	**Adult role:** Discuss the children's creations with them. Encourage reflection. **Enhancement:** Eggshell.
Painting		
Playdough		
Construction		
Grassed area	Lack of understanding of the concept of 'bouncing'.	**Adult role:** Encourage the children to attempt to bounce the different objects. Ask them to think about why some bounce and others do not. **Enhancement:** Various objects made out of different materials.

Figure 6: Environment enhancement plan for continuous provision during the all about eggs project

Listening and documenting

In Reggio Emilia it is recognised that children have different "forms of expression" that are influenced by their individual learning styles (Thornton and Brunton, 2007, p.77). Children express themselves through various mediums such as their play and conversation, as well as the writing, pictures, models and sculptures they create. Observation is an "integral daily part of the practitioner's role" (DCELLS, 2008b, p.22) that helps "everyone to see how the children's thinking is developing" (DCSF, 2007, Principles into Practice Card 4.3), and ensures the "children's needs and interests lead the learning" (CCEA, 2007, p.10). **It is by observing and documenting the children's various modes of expression that practitioners are able to truly listen to and respond to the needs and interests of the children (Rinaldi, 1998).**

It follows that it is necessary to plan observations carefully and ensure that an adequate number of staff members are allocated to the task. Furthermore, it is crucial that practitioners keep an open mind when observing and be as receptive as possible to different or unusual ideas. Remaining objective is difficult because 'in the act of choosing what to observe and record, the observer selects what is meaningful to them' (Thornton and Brunton, 2009, p.101). This is especially important to bear in mind considering that projects are meant to follow the interests of the children, rather than an adult agenda.

Observations are taken of all aspects of project work; the children's free play, adult-led focused activities and adult-supported group investigations. At the beginning when the children first encounter a provocation, practitioners observe and note down their reactions, comments and conversations. At this stage it is likely that there will be a significant amount of interest and bustle and so it is preferable to have as many practitioners as possible on this task. **When the children are brought together for a discussion or mind-mapping session it is helpful for one practitioner to lead the discussion, while another records the children's ideas and questions and keeps additional notes of anything else significant.** At this stage practitioners only need blank paper and post-it notes and should aim to record as much information as possible. As a project progresses and the children become involved in adult-led investigations and independent explorations, more detailed and comprehensive observations are carried

out. Practitioners write down what the children say and do; keep records of their conversations and questions; photograph and/or film their activities; and collect photographs or photocopies of the work they produce.

Focused observations

In the case of the all about eggs project, practitioners were assigned to the different areas of provision around the setting and asked to undertake focused written and photographic observations of any project-related activities that the children were involved in. Practitioners focused on one particular child at a time and closely observed and recorded their activities for up to 20 minutes. Figure 8 is an example of a focused written observation taken of a little girl examining and discussing a boiled egg in the investigation area.

Photographic observations are particularly useful because they cut out the need to set the context with written description, saving time and enabling practitioners to focus in greater detail upon the children's conversations and behaviours. Jenkinson Evans (2010) offers some advice about how to take photographs that provide a deeper insight into children's learning. She suggests:

- crouching to a lower level so that photographs are more representative of a child's perspective;

- zooming in to get close up photographs that capture facial expressions; and

- taking photographs from a variety of angles in order to provide an overview of the learning situation, e.g. types of resources available, other children or adults involved and layout of the setting.

Figure 9 is an example of a focused photographic observation taken of a little girl playing with a plate of eggshell she found in the craft area.

Snapshot observations

Snapshot observations enable practitioners to keep a quick note of any interesting occurrences during the day. They are also particularly useful for recording comments made by the children during focused activities (see Figure 7 for examples).

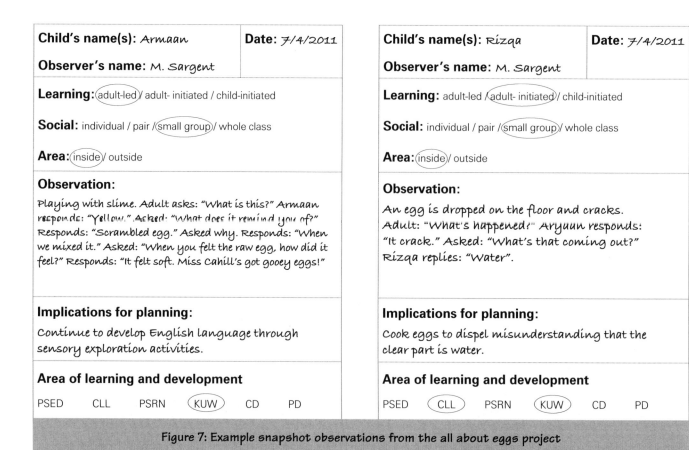

Child's name(s): Armaan	Date: 7/4/2011
Observer's name: M. Sargent	

Learning: (adult-led)/ adult- initiated / child-initiated

Social: individual / pair /(small group)/ whole class

Area: (inside)/ outside

Observation:

Playing with slime. Adult asks: "What is this?" Armaan responds: "Yellow." Asked: "What does it remind you of?" Responds: "Scrambled egg." Asked why. Responds: "When we mixed it." Asked: "When you felt the raw egg, how did it feel?" Responds: "It felt soft. Miss Cahill's got gooey eggs!"

Implications for planning:

Continue to develop English language through sensory exploration activities.

Area of learning and development

PSED   CLL   PSRN   (KUW)   CD   PD

Child's name(s): Rizqa	Date: 7/4/2011
Observer's name: M. Sargent	

Learning: adult-led /(adult- initiated)/ child-initiated

Social: individual / pair /(small group)/ whole class

Area: (inside)/ outside

Observation:

An egg is dropped on the floor and cracks. Adult: "What's happened?" Aryuun responds: "It crack." Asked: "What's that coming out?" Rizqa replies: "Water".

Implications for planning:

Cook eggs to dispel misunderstanding that the clear part is water.

Area of learning and development

PSED   (CLL)   PSRN   (KUW)   CD   PD

Figure 7: Example snapshot observations from the all about eggs project

Digital recordings

Digital filming and audio recording are also effective observation methods for a number of reasons. First, they help to capture a detailed and accurate record of events. Written notes are only as precise and comprehensive as an observer is able to produce. Conversations can be complicated and fast flowing, making them difficult to write down. Filming and recording makes it possible to accurately capture children's comments and conversations. In addition, film makes it possible to record physical movements and facial expressions that may be missed while an observer is concentrating on the page. Filming and recording also help to free up the practitioner to interact with the children. Without the need to write everything down, the practitioner can actively listen to the children, ask useful questions and engage them in sustained shared thinking. Furthermore, the recordings make it possible for practitioners to revisit their observations a number of times with different focuses in mind.

During the all about eggs project filming was found to be especially helpful when observing the adult-supported investigation into breaking eggs. While one practitioner took the role of guide and questioner, another was allocated the role of observer, filming and taking written notes. Filming enabled practitioners to focus in on individual children as they smashed the eggs but also to see the reactions of the other children in the group as they looked on. In addition, as the children gathered around the tray to feel the raw egg, the film allowed the practitioners to pick out interesting observations about individuals from amongst the fast-paced activity and excitement of the group.

Work samples

As well as practitioner observations, the pieces of work that the children produce can be documented. For example, any drawings or paintings the children create in response to the project can be photocopied and annotated with comments from the children. In addition, any models the children make can be photographed. These are helpful records for practitioners to revisit alongside their observations.

Focused written observation record: All About Eggs Project

Child's name(s): Afraha

Observer's name: F. Younis

Area of provision/focused activity: Adult-initiated – KUW investigation area – raw and cooked eggs

Date: 7/4/2011

Start time: 12.20 pm

End time: 12.40 pm

Observation notes (children's actions, comments and conservation):

Afraha looks at all the eggs but takes most interest in the peeled boiled egg. Holds it in her hand – seems to be feeling it. "It feels cold," she says. She holds it in her hand and looks at another egg. Picks up a magnifier and looks at the egg in her hand. "Oh look it's cracking," she says. (There is a small hair on the egg.) "It's taking a long time to crack," she says. She and Zoha continue to examine the egg, looking at it with magnifiers and pointing to the 'crack'. Afraha walks away. She comes back and picks up the egg and checks it with a magnifying glass. "Oh, it's ok. It's not cracked yet." Turns to Zoha. "Let's go get a knife to cut it." Both girls go to the playdough table and come back without a knife. They go back to the playdough table again and come back without a knife again.

Area of learning and development (PSED) CLL PSRN (KUW) CD PD

Thoughts/questions:

Afraha is looking for a crack in a boiled and shelled egg.

Waiting for it to hatch? Understanding concepts?

Notes from shared reflection:

Perhaps the girls did not feel that they could use a knife from the playdough area – do the children feel that they cannot transfer resources from one area to another?

Later with Zoha – they were waiting for a chick to come out.

Implications for planning:

Provide knives in the investigation area for cutting into eggs.

Ensure that children know they can find and transfer resources to different areas independently.

Find out why chicks come out of some eggs and not others. Incubate some chicken eggs.

Figure 8: Focused written observation record from the all about eggs project.

Focused written observation record: All About Eggs Project

Child's name(s): Sarah

Observer's name: Z. Saddiq

Area of provision/focused activity: Child-initiated play – craft area/Home corner

Date: 8/4/2011

Start time: 12.50 pm

End time: 1.10 pm

Observation notes (children's actions, comments and conservation):

Sarah tried some eggshells from a plate onto the table. She takes a knife from the investigation table and uses it to cut them up. She puts the knife down and tries with her hands. I mention that using knife will stop her hurting her fingers. She picks up the knife again and continues. She tells me, "I'm cutting egg. I'm making an egg cream." She collects the shells and puts them back on the plate. "I'm putting it in the oven." She carries the plate to the home corner. She mixes the shells on the plate with a spoon. "I'm going to put it in now." She puts the plate in the oven and turns knob on cooker. Takes plate out of the oven. "I'm going to make the babies eat cake."

Area of learning and development

PSED   CLL   PSRN   (KUW)   CD   PD

Thoughts/questions:

Preparing a meal? Had a clear idea of what she was doing.

Responded to my suggestion to use the knife instead of fingers.

Notes from shared reflection:

Perhaps Sarah chose to use the eggshell in cooking role-play because it was on a plate rather than just on the table.

Mum mentioned Sarah's interest in cooking at home – own cooking pots and pans. Copies mum and helps with cooking as well.

Implications for planning:

Develop the role-play cooking resources in the home corner (egg boxes etc). Mount photographs of eggs cooking in different ways on the walls.

Figure 9: Focused photographic observation record from the all about eggs project.

Reflecting upon and discussing documentation

The documentation collected throughout a project is constantly reflected upon and discussed both among practitioners and between practitioners and children, and parents too. The findings and conclusions from these discussions inform ongoing planning. **By taking this time to reflect upon, discuss, interpret and use observations, practitioners acknowledge the centrality of the child in the educational process.**

Discussion between practitioners and with parents

Thornton and Brunton suggest that when observing, practitioners should constantly remind themselves to focus upon the "process of learning" rather than what the children produce (2009, p.121). The observation record sheets used during the all about eggs project were designed with this in mind. They remind practitioners to record children's actions, comments and conversation and encourage analysis by providing space for writing down any thoughts or questions that come to mind during the observation. Noting these emerging ideas as they occur is useful for later discussion and reflection. Sharing observations with others helps to "eliminate subjectivity" (Jenkinson Evans, 2010, p.xvi). Other practitioners will present different views and perspectives that help to build a more rounded picture. They may also be able to bring additional information about the children to the discussion. The Welsh Foundation Phase Framework highlights the importance of including all staff in such discussions: "Time should be made for the team to engage in reflective practice as this leads to greater understanding of child development, how children learn, the needs of children and how best to meet those needs" (DCELLS, 2008b, p.24). Of course, it is the parents who know their children best and they will often be able to offer interesting information that sheds an interesting light on observations.

Figure 7 provides an example of the benefit of this process. This was the first focused observation taken of Sarah. A second observation was later taken of her playing with a jug and whisk in a tray of slime. She described it as being similar to something purple that her mum makes for her to eat with a biscuit at home. It seemed that the project about eggs directly appealed to Sarah's preoccupation with cooking. When reflecting upon this with another practitioner, it was discovered that Angel Delight had been used in the malleable area in the past. Another practitioner explained that Sarah has a special diet due to health reasons. Furthermore, reflection with Sarah's mum revealed she often helps to prepare food at home and has her own pots and pans for role-play cooking as well. It was decided that the role-play cooking resources should be developed to enable Sarah to further explore this interest in relation to eggs.

Reflecting upon learning with children

Sharing documentation with the children is equally as important because it promotes "ownership" over learning (Scottish Government, 2010, p.5). Children who are "actively involved in planning, reviewing and reflecting upon what they have done" gain a clearer understanding of what they have learned so far and what they need to do to further this (CCEA, 2006, p.4): Teaching means systematically helping children to learn so that they make connections in their learning, are actively led forward, and can reflect on their learning. (DCSF, 2007, Principles into Practice Card 2.3). This is a democratic approach to teaching and learning that supports the active involvement of the child in the educational process (Rinaldi, 2001; Maynard and Chicken, 2010).

Photographic observations and digital video recordings are particularly useful for encouraging reflection in young children because they provide a visual stimulus for discussion. Photographs of the children involved in their investigations can be mounted on low-level displays for the children to see and video footage can be played back to individuals or a large group on an interactive whiteboard. Practitioners can bring children to the screen or display for discussion or observe the children talking about the photographs or film between themselves. When engaging a child in reflection it is useful to try and do this as soon as possible after the activity while it is still fresh in their mind. When watching a film of an activity it can help to turn the volume down in the first instance and ask the child to explain what is happening. This prevents them from simply repeating what is said on the film. The film can then be played back again with sound so that the child can listen to what was said and reflect upon this as well.

Figure 10 is an example of the record sheet designed for reflection and used during the all about eggs project. A list of open-ended questions were printed on the back of the sheet for the practitioner to refer to as prompts for discussion. The example highlights the value of reflecting in this way, in terms of helping the child to consolidate their learning and enabling the practitioner to assess knowledge and understanding.

Discussing work samples also allows children to explain their thought processes and helps them to reflect upon what they have produced (see Figure 11).

Interpreting documentation to inform planning

After reflecting upon, sharing and discussing documentation, practitioners consider the implications for the ongoing planning and development of the provocation or project. Space is allocated on planning and observation documents to prompt practitioners to

think about and note down their thoughts and ideas in this respect (see Figures 4 to 11). The planning is then revisited and added to or amended accordingly. The project continues and the process begins all over again.

For example, the documentation collected during the all about eggs project was used formatively throughout to plan ongoing activities and learning environment enhancements. Figure 12 on page 61 illustrates how the observations of the children informed the planning as the project progressed.

Table 1 on page 63 illustrates how a full-scale project might be organised on a day-to-day basis. It explains the role of the practitioner throughout and illustrates how the cyclical process of planning, observation, reflection, discussion and interpretation works in practice.

A simple provocation is developed in very much the same way. Any observations that lead to significant planning developments or alterations can be recorded on a working planning document and kept alongside the original open-ended planning. Figure 13 on page 64 is an example of the working planning document used during the cocoon provocation.

Practitioners can bring children to photograph displays for reflection

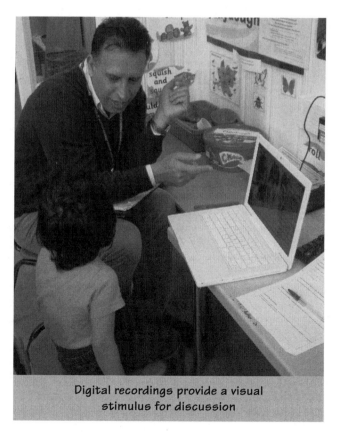

Digital recordings provide a visual stimulus for discussion

Providing guidance and support

While the children are involved in their explorations and investigations, practitioners are on hand to offer guidance and support. Providing the tools, materials and resources the children need is a relatively straightforward task. However, providing the guidance the children need to develop their investigative and critical thinking skills is much more difficult.

Helm and Katz (2001) explain that rather than give children information, practitioners should give them time and space to obtain it for themselves. Practitioners can help with this by facilitating discussion, encouraging children to talk together and ask questions of each other as well as adults. They can also help by offering to clarify information and clear up inaccuracies and misconceptions.

The extent to which the children will be able to engage themselves in meaningful investigation will depend upon the age, needs and ability of the children, as well as whether they are used to directing their own work and play. **Younger children and those who are new to the project approach will need much more guidance and support.** Those who have previous experience of project work will already be used to working independently, managing their time and selecting resources with specific aims in mind.

Digital observation record: All About Eggs Project	**Date:** 8/4/2011

Child's name(s): Humam

Observer's name: M. Sargent

Observation context: Film recording of breaking eggs investigation

Practitioner's initial thoughts, questions and ideas about the recording:

Humam doesn't seem to understand the concept of 'bouncing'. Tries to bounce it and it smashes but he answers "yes" when asked if it bounced.

He was very excited about the egg smashing.

Unsure about concept of 'hard' and 'soft'.

Notes from shared reflection with other practitioners:

Humam has since spoken about the activity and remembered trying to bounce the egg. Talked about how the egg 'breaked'.

He remembered while watching the recording that he wanted to bounce the egg.

Notes from shared reflection with the children:

While watching the recording Humam said, "I cracked the egg first."

He got excited and exclaimed, "It went like this..." and stamped on the floor with his foot.

Implications for planning:

Humam was excited by this activity. Plan more hands-on investigations like this that help to develop sensory concepts such as 'hard', 'soft' and bounce

> **Figure 10: Digital observation record from the all about eggs project**

Record of reflection and discussion about work produced:

All About Eggs Project

Date: 6/4/2011

Child's name(s): Jamal

Observer's name: M. Sargent

Observation context: Child-initiated play during free-flow time

Practitioner's initial thoughts, questions and ideas about the piece of work:

Jamal made Humpty Dumpty at the craft table by cutting out an egg shape and sticking paper strips on as limbs.

Seems that Jamal noticed Easter egg templates and made a connection.

Notes from shared reflection with other practitioners:

Some children don't understand the meaning of the word 'crack' - could do something to demonstrate this.

Notes from shared reflection with the children:

Asked Jamal: "What happens to Humpty Dumpty?" Responds: "He falls off the wall and cracks."

Asked "Do you think you would crack if you fell off the wall?"

Responds: "No" and laughs.

Asked: "Why not?" Jamal shrugs shoulders.

Asked: "What is HD made of?" Responds: "Eggs."

Asked: "Why do you think the egg cracked when it fell?" Jamal shrugs his shoulders.

Implications for planning:

Investgiate how and why eggs crack when dropped/thrown etc.

Find out the meaning of the word 'crack' and think of synonyms.

Figure 11: Record of reflection and discussion about work produced during the all about eggs project

As previously mentioned, the nursery children at Horton Grange need a high level of adult support and guidance, especially language modeling to enable them to internalise information and develop their knowledge and understanding in different subjects. The children's language needs significantly impact upon the extent to which they are able to embark upon independent investigation and practitioners had to work closely with them throughout the all about eggs project. This affected the ratio of adult-led to child-initiated activities that were able to take place. A number of adult-led focused activities were necessary to help the children develop their language and vocabulary. There was also a need for a greater level of adult support and guidance during the group investigation, which limited its scope in terms of how far it could organically evolve. This should be compared to the cocoon provocation, which was carried out with a class of reception-age children who are more independent and do not have the same language needs.

Figure 12: An example of the use of observation to inform ongoing planning during the all about eggs project

Observations of the children's reactions to raw egg led practitioners to introduce slime to the water tray

Promoting sustained shared thinking

A large part of the practitioner's role during a project is asking open questions that encourage creative and critical thinking skills. This is a difficult skill that takes time and practice to develop and is made easier by including question ideas on planning and observation documents. It is also a good idea to display reminders around the learning environment that will serve as prompts for all practitioners. This can be done in the following ways:

Display open questions both indoors and outside

It is useful to display general open questions around the learning environment, both inside and outdoors. These serve as prompts for practitioners who are seeking to develop a conversation with a child in order to help further their thinking. The questions are intended to act as inspiration for practitioners, who need only glance up for a moment to get an idea about what to ask next. They also serve as useful prompts for additional adults such as students, parents and support staff, who might be

There's not enough time in the day

Issues and concerns

Early years practitioners are under a great deal of pressure to meet varying demands from different sources. They may feel that project work is just something else to fit into an already packed timetable.

The all about eggs project demonstrates how project work can be integrated into a very busy timetable. The planning in this setting is complex and eventful, and the project had to be worked around this. Rather than view project work as another initiative to fit in, it is useful to view it in terms of how it can help to reduce workload in other areas. For instance, as each of the examples in this book demonstrate, project work provides opportunities for learning in a variety of subject areas. This means there is less of a need to plan specific subject-based adult-led activities. Furthermore, the documentation collected during a single project will provide practitioners with a great deal of information about a large number of children. This helps to reduce the number of targeted observations needed to ascertain individual levels of achievement in particular areas. Rather than being onerous and time consuming, project work makes it possible to fit more into the day.

new to the setting. Some ideas for open-ended questions are:

- What are you doing?

- What do you think that means?

- How do you feel about...?

- Can you explain how it works?

- What might you do next time?

- Why do you think that?

Stage in project	Practitioners' roles
Initial encounter and investigation of the provocation	Support sustained shared thinking: ■ Listen ■ Prompt discussion ■ Ask questions ■ Encourage children to question Observe and record: ■ Film explorations and discussions ■ Take photographic and written observations of children's responses to the provocation ■ Record children's comments and questions that arise during group discussions Reflect: ■ Gather the children to share their experiences of the provocation
Finding out what the children know and would like to learn Producing initial plans	Discuss: ■ Gather the children together and create spidergrams recording their thoughts and ideas about the provocation. Find out where there are gaps in their knowledge and what they would like to find out more about Discuss: ■ Meet together to share observations and spidergrams ■ Choose resources and activities that will enhance the learning environment and help children to develop interests ■ Plan initial adult-led focused activities to address gaps in knowledge ■ Choose a focus for adult-supported investigation Document: ■ Begin to display documentation and planning in view of children, practitioners and visitors
Enhancements of learning environment in place, focused activities and adult-supported investigation set up	Support sustained shared thinking: ■ Listen ■ Prompt discussion ■ Ask questions ■ Encourage children to question Observe and record: ■ Take film, photographic and written observations Document: ■ Continue to display documentation for adults and children Reflect and discuss: ■ Share the observations with the adults and discuss ■ Share with children so they can reflect upon what they are learning
Development of the learning environment and adult-supported investigation	Continue to support sustained shared thinking, take observations, document and reflect upon learning. Reflect and develop: ■ Support children's investigations by giving them time and space to indulge in their self-directed activities ■ Refer to observations and facilitate children's learning by providing relevant resources to extend their activities
Conclusion and evaluation	Document: ■ Complete displays and create a learning story about the project to share with children, practitioners and visitors Reflect: ■ Use the display or learning story to aid reflection with (a) the children to help them reflect upon what they have learned and what more they would have liked to do, and (b) practitioners to reflect upon what has been learned about the children and the implications of the project outcomes for future planning

Table 1: Overview of a full-scale project

Foundation - Summer 1 - Minibeasts Cocoon Provocation - Ongoing planning	
Observation notes	**Plan to go forward**
Week 1 (WB 23/04/07) Thursday - Cocoon noticed immediately. Children were excited and everything got a bit chaotic. Unable to hear children speaking.	Make changes to cocoon at more convenient times. Gather children together and split into talk partners to share ideas and views - should make observation easier.
Week 2 (WB 30/04/07) Wednesday – Children noticed blue antennae sticking out of cocoon. This prompted discussion about they type of creature inside. Thursday – Cocoon fully hatched but children reluctant to bring creature down from cocoon because worried about him. Friday – Children decided creature can come down but should be given time to get used to noisy classroom before joining in. Lots of interest in drawing pictures of creature.	Provide books and pictures of creatures that are similar in colour or have legs/antennae of the same shape to help children with investigations. Help children to find out which creatures create cocoons. Leave creature in cocoon and discuss this further tomorrow morning. Ensure plenty of opportunity at the beginning of next week to continue this.
Week 3 (WB 08/05/07) Children point out that they recognise the creature as Flik from 'A Bug's Life'. Had to make up cover story involving an uncle in America. Children want to let Uncle Flik know that Tom is ok.	Focus on letter writing this week and help children to write to Uncle Flik. Create a letter from Uncle Flik in response. Ask Paula to bring it down to class at the beginning of next week.

Figure 13: Working planning document for the cocoon provocation

- What do you think about…?

- Is there anything you would like to say about…?

- What do you think will happen next?

- What do you think this is for?

- What do you think is happening?

- How can we make this better?

- What would you do if…?

- What do you mean by that?

- Why is this important to you?

- What would happen if…?

- Who agrees with…?

- What would you like to ask?

- Is there anything you would like to talk about?

- How do you know about…?

- Have you ever seen…?

Create sustained shared thinking cards

It is also helpful to display cards that promote sustained shared thinking in each area of provision within the setting. These cards have suggestions for open-ended questions and useful key words that can be introduced into conversation. In addition, the cards might highlight where such activities fit into the curriculum. These cards are available on the accompanying CD-Rom.

Set up informative displays

Informative displays set at the children's eye level are also an effective way to prompt discussion. Such displays might feature posters or photographs with snippets of information and questions about the project theme. These displays can be used to provide information and stimulate conversation about a subject. Helm and Katz (2001) further suggest mounting children's questions for investigation in the relevant areas of provision around the setting. In addition, photographic observations can be displayed along with captions and quotations taken from the children. Practitioners can use these to help the children talk about their investigations and reflect upon what they have been doing. In addition, children can be involved in setting up displays that show others what they have learned.

Key points

- **The role of the practitioner consists of three main tasks:**

    - **Listening to the children and documenting their learning;**

    - **Reflecting upon, discussing and interpreting this documentation to inform ongoing planning;**

    - **Providing resources and intellectual guidance during investigative work.**

- **Observations are taken of all aspects of project work; the children's free play, adult-led focused activities and adult-supported group investigations.**

- **The documentation collected is constantly reflected upon and discussed both among practitioners and between practitioners and children, and parents too. The findings and conclusions from these discussions inform ongoing planning.**

- **Practitioners provide guidance during investigative work by facilitating discussion, encouraging children to talk together and ask questions of each other as well as adults. This is referred to as sustaining shared thinking.**

Concluding the project

There are a number of factors that might determine when a project should come to an end. It may be that it naturally concludes because the children are no longer interested and begin moving onto other activities. It could be that external factors and time

restraints mean that a project can only ever last for a specific duration. Otherwise, as Helm and Katz (2001) point out, it might be that moving the investigation any further would involve skills that are beyond the children's current capabilities. Whatever the reason, it is a good idea to end the project with an activity that brings closure and helps the children to reflect upon and share what they have learned. This section looks at some ideas for closing activities.

Reflecting upon what has been learned

The conclusion of a project is a valuable opportunity to involve children in reflection upon what they have learned through their investigations. Helm and Katz explain that this is best done by involving the children in "culminating activities" that help them to look back on the project and consolidate their learning (2001, p.51). They make several suggestions for various closing activities. Some of these and others are considered and discussed below.

Revisiting the mind-map

Perhaps the simplest idea is to show the children the original mind-map that they contributed to at the beginning of the project. The practitioner can read out some of the questions and ask the children if they now know the answers. The practitioner can also read out some comments and ask the children for any responses they might have in light of their newly acquired knowledge. The practitioner can then either add to the original mind-map using a different coloured marker or create a new mind-map detailing what the children have learned. This is an effective visual way of showing the children how their knowledge and understanding has grown (see Figure 15 on page 66).

Revisiting the provocation

Revisiting the original provocation can also generate discussion about what the children have found out since the project began. For example, look again at the interesting object or picture and ask the children to share what they know about it or how it makes them feel now; if the provocation was a visit or event, share a book of photographs and encourage the children to think back to why it was so interesting and what they have learned from it; or go back to the original question and ask the children to draw on their investigative experience to offer some answers. This helps the children to recognise project work as a learning vehicle and a way of furthering their knowledge about something.

Reviewing documentation

Observations and work produced can be revisited as a way of reminding the children of their thought processes throughout the project. Practitioners can read out written observations, show photographs or play video back to the children. Several snapshots highlighting where a change of opinion has occurred or how some new knowledge has been acquired will help to demonstrate to the children how learning takes place.

Sharing a learning story

A learning story can be created from observation material and read back to the children (Bayley, 2006). The idea here is to tell the story of the project from the very beginning, showing and telling the children what happened. Learning stories can be presented in a variety of ways. For example, practitioners can use presentation software to project chronologically arranged photographs with observation quotes or dictated notes from the children. A story could otherwise be presented as a picture book or arranged as a comic strip with speech bubbles and an accompanying narrative. Learning stories are also a useful way of communicating projects to parents. They can either be duplicated and sent home or displayed in the parents' area of the setting. The learning story produced for the all about eggs project can be found on the CD-Rom as an example.

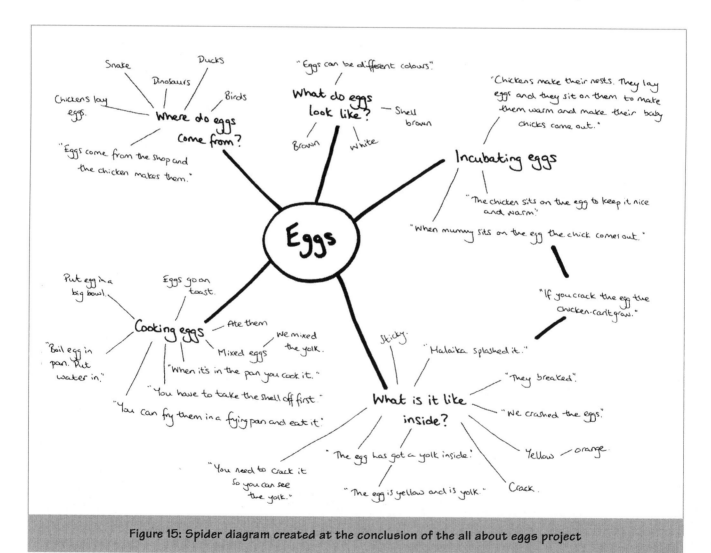

Figure 15: Spider diagram created at the conclusion of the all about eggs project

A large-scale display of documentation presents an overview of the project

role. Furthermore, for managers and leaders, it provides evidence of learning and proof of good practice. Small-scale displays can also be created in conjunction with the children. These could feature, for example, photographs from the project with captions dictated by the children.

Creating a book

Another idea is to create a book of the project. Unlike a learning story, which is created by the practitioner, this book is created in conjunction with the children. It contains examples of children's work as well as photographs, with captions and stories dictated by the children. For example, a book featuring the all about eggs project might open with some photographs from the farm visit, captioned with some of the children's initial questions about eggs. It may contain some pictures created by the children, for instance the Humpty Dumpty made by Jamal. It could also show some photographs taken during the egg smashing investigation or cooking activity with a brief commentary supplied by the children about what they did and what happened.

Sharing what has been learned

It is useful for children to share what they have learned with others. This is beneficial to the children because it is another way of reflecting upon and consolidating what they have learned. It is also useful for practitioners because it enables them to assess what the children have learned from the project and how this has improved their knowledge, skills and understanding. Furthermore, it is a way of presenting learning to parents, managers and auditors. Katz and Chard (2000) suggest some ideas for sharing project learning and these are considered and elaborated below.

Show and tell

Some children may feel confident enough to show and tell. In this case, practitioners can help the children set up low-level displays or computer presentations about various aspects of the project. Three-dimensional displays of art and craftwork can also be set up. Children from other classes or settings, as well as parents can be invited in to hear about the project directly from the children. Again, using the all about eggs project as an example here, it would be a nice idea to set up a number of displays around the setting featuring different aspects of the project. Children could then be posted at each display to talk to the visitors. For instance, a tabletop display could be set up with eggs cooked in different ways alongside the cooking equipment used. The children here could explain how each of the eggs were cooked and how they tasted. A further display of photographs of different eggs and the birds that lay them could also be mounted. The children here could tell the visitors which eggs come from which bird and what the eggs look like inside when cracked. Also, a film taken during the smashing eggs activity

Displaying documentation

Displaying documentation is useful for a number of reasons. For practitioners, a large-scale display of planning samples and observation notes presents an overview of how the provocation or project developed. This is also a useful way of offering an insight into foundation stage practice for visitors and parents because it tells the story of the children's learning and illustrates the practitioner's could be set to play on the interactive whiteboard. The children here could talk about what it was like to smash the eggs, what happened when they did and how it made them feel to do it. Of course setting up something like this would involve a great deal of preparation and practice before hand and the children may need considerable support.

Key points

◾ **It is a good idea to end the project with an activity that brings closure and helps the children to reflect upon and share what they have learned.**

◾ **Children can be helped to reflect upon what they have learned by revisiting the original mind-map from the beginning of the project; revisiting the original provocation; reviewing observations and work produced; or sharing a learning story that tells about what happened during the project from beginning to end.**

◾ **Projects can be shared with others by creating displays and/or books containing photographs, observation extracts and pieces of the children's work. Some children may feel confident enough to show and tell.**

Sneha broke a duck's egg. She explained that eggshell is "like glasses" because "they break" if they are dropped as well.

Usman used a knife to cut up, mash and mix some raw and cooked eggs together.

A page from the all about eggs learning story

Part Three: Communicating the project approach

This final section is intended as a guide for leaders and managers of early years settings, as well as trainers. It aims to provide some guidance and resources to help communicate to others how to use the project approach, as well as the theory behind it. Practitioners or students might also like to use the resources provided here to reflect upon what they have read in the book and consolidate what they have learned. This section should be used in conjunction with the resources on the CD-Rom attached to the front of the book.

Explaining the rationale behind the approach

When communicating the project approach to others it is useful to explain the rationale behind it. Practitioners will be more comfortable with an approach if they understand the theory and research that underpins it. The first part of this book looks at how the approach fosters particular aspects of educational practice that support effective early learning. The main points have been summarised and put together to create a presentation, The Rationale Behind the Project Approach, which can be found on the CD-Rom. This presentation sets the scene and provides a context for a further training session about the practical aspects of planning and carrying out provocations and projects. The slides feature diagrams that aim to simplify the theory and make it more accessible. The presentation is also concluded with a summary of key points. It would be useful to print this presentation out for trainees to annotate during the training.

The Rationale Behind the Project Approach presentation

Demonstrating how the approach works in practice

A second presentation entitled Planning and Carrying out Projects is also provided on the CD-Rom. This is intended as a more interactive resource that encourages trainees to get involved and experience the approach first-hand while providing a step-by-step explanation of how provocations and projects are carried out. The following is a suggestion for how the training session might be organised.

Planning and Carrying out Projects presentation

Resources needed

■ Some unusual objects

■ Clipboards, paper and pens

■ Large sheets of paper and marker pens

■ Digital cameras

■ Easy access to a number of computers and a printer

■ Scissors and glue

■ Training handouts from the CD-Rom

Training handouts and learning story from the all about eggs project

The training presentation 'Planning and Carrying out Projects' features examples from the all about eggs project

Practitioners need to understand their role in developing their project

The training

This training is best delivered in the early years setting, where the trainees have access to a range of resources. Divide the trainees into groups of no more than ten. Split the groups into two: investigators and observers. Give out the training hand outs from the CD-Rom.

Start with a provocation

■ Refer to Slides 2 to 5 to explain what a provocation is, the difference between a simple provocation and a full-scale project, and how a project is planned (see page 6 for an explanation of this).

■ Give the investigators an interesting object that will provoke discussion and debate. This might be an easily recognisable object with complex design features or something unusual that has no clear purpose.

■ Give the observers clipboards, paper and pens.

■ Refer the groups to the instructions in their handouts and give them 10 minutes to complete Task 1.

■ Give the trainees 10 minutes to complete Task 2.

Explain the initial planning process

■ Refer to Slides 6 to 12 to explain the process involved in planning a simple provocation or full-scale project (as explained on pages 41 to 51).

■ Merge the paired groups together and give them 30 minutes to complete Task 3.

■ Give the merged groups a further 20 minutes to complete Task 4.

Explain the practitioner's role in developing a project

■ Refer to Slides 13 and 14 to explain the practitioner's role and the cyclical process of observation, reflection/discussion, interpretation and ongoing planning (as explained on page 41).

■ Refer to Slides 15 to 18 to explain the observation sheets (as explained on pages 53 to 56).

- Split the groups into investigators and observers again and give them 30 minutes to complete Task 5.

- Merge the paired groups together and give them 10 minutes to complete Task 6.

- Refer to Slides 19 and 20 to explain about digital observation and collecting work samples (as explained on page 54).

- Refer back to Slides 10 and 11 and point out the implications for planning sections, to show where observations were used to inform the all about eggs project planning.

- Ask the merged groups to refer to their own observations and go back to their initial investigation plan. Give them time to make alterations and additions.

- Sum up by referring to the table in the hand out presenting an overview of a full-scale project.

This would be a good time to break.

Talk about how to promote sustained shared thinking

- Refer to Slide 21 to explain the practitioner's role as a guide and support during the investigative process (as explained on pages 59 and 60).

- Refer to Slides 22 to 26 to explain how practitioners can promote creative and critical thinking skills during project work (as explained on pages 62 to 65).

Explain how a project is concluded

- Refer to Slides 27 to 29 to explain the importance of reflecting upon the project and provide some ideas about how to do so with concluding activities (as explained on pages 65 to 68).

- Refer to the learning story from the all about eggs project as an example.

Note

Both presentations are fairly comprehensive and detailed, with references to all four British early years curriculum documents. Although they can be used in their present form they are intended as adaptable resources that can be edited according to individual purpose and need. The presentations have also been annotated for extra guidance.

Note

The activities described involve trainees observing one another. Therefore, it is a good idea to allow them to form their own groups and allocate the roles of observer and investigator themselves. Explain that the purpose of the observations is to find out what interests the investigator and what questions they have about the object. There should be no value judgements made. This should help to create a safe learning environment in which the investigators feel comfortable being observed.

Further information

Examples of projects in action

Edwards C, Gandini L, Forman G (1998) *The Hundred Languages of Children*. 2nd edn. Ablex Publishing

Helm JH, Katz L (2001) *Young Investigators: The Project Approach in the Early Years*. Teachers College Press

Katz L, SC Chard (2000) *Engaging Children's Minds: The Project Approach*. 2nd edn. USA, Ablex Publishing

Ideas for provocations and projects

Bayley R, L Broadbent (2002) *Helping Young Children to Think Creatively*. Lawrence Educational Publications

Featherstone S (2003) *The Little Book of Investigations*. A&C Black

Featherstone S (2010) *The Little Book of Explorations*. A&C Black

Information about schemas and how to identify them

Athey C (2007) *Extending Thought in Young Children*. 2nd edn. Sage

Bruce T (2005) *Early Childhood Education*. 3rd edn. Hodder Arnold

Louis S, Beswick C, Magraw L et al (2008) *Again, Again! Understanding Schemas in Young Children*. Featherstone Education

Guidance on observation

Hobart C, Frankel J, Walker M (2009) *A Practical Guide to Child Observation and Assessment*. 4th edn. Nelson Thornes

Ridall-Leech S (2008) *How to Observe Children*. 2nd edn. Heinemann

Promoting sustained shared thinking

Call N, Featherstone S (2003) *The Thinking Child*. Network Educational Press

Charlesworth V (2004) *Helping Young Children to Ask Questions*. Lawrence Educational Publications

Charlesworth V (2005) *Critical Skills in the Early Years*. Network Educational Press

Clarke J, (2007) *Sustaining Shared Thinking*. Featherstone Education

Dowling M (2005) *Supporting Young Children's Sustained Shared Thinking: An Exploration*. The British Association for Early Childhood Education

References

Books

Anning A (2005) Play and legislated curriculum. Back to basics: an alternative view. In: Moyles J ed, *The Excellence of Play*. 2nd edn. Berkshire, Open University Press

Bayley R, Broadbent L (2002) *Helping Young Children to Think Creatively*. Walsall, Lawrence Educational Publications

Bredekamp S, Copple C, eds (1997) *Developmentally Appropriate Practice in Early Childhood Programs*. Revised edition. Washington DC, National Association for the Education of Young Children

Broadhead P (2004) *Early Years Play and Learning: Developing Social Skills and Cooperation*. London, Routledge Falmer

Broadhead P, English C (2005) Open-ended role play: supporting creativity and developing identity. In: Moyes J, ed, *The Excellence of Play*. 2nd edn. Berkshire, Open University Press

Bruce T (2005) *Early Childhood Education*. 3rd edn. London, Hodder Arnold

Bruner J (1960) *The Process of Education*. Cambridge, MA, Harvard University Press

Bruner J (1966) *Toward a Theory of Instruction*. Cambridge, MA, Harvard University Press

Charlesworth V (2005) *Critical Skills in the Early Years*. Stafford, Network Educational Press

Clarke J (2007) *Sustaining Shared Thinking*. Lutterworth, Featherstone Education

Cooper J (2010) *The Early Years Communication Handbook*. London, Practical Pre-School Books

Csikszentmihalyi M (1992) *Flow: The Psychology of Happiness*. London, Random House

Csikszentmihalyi M (1998) The flow experience and its significance for human psychology. In: Csikszentmihalyi M and Csikszentmihalyi IS. eds, *Optimal Experience: Psychological Studies of Flow in Consciousness*. Cambridge, Cambridge University Press

Donaldson M (1978) *Children's Minds*. Glasgow, Fontana Press

Duffy B (2010) Using creativity and creative learning to enrich the lives of young children at the Thomas Coram Centre. In: Tims C, ed, *Born Creative*. London, Demos. Available from: http://www.demos.co.uk/publications/born-creative-

Edwards C (1998) Partner, nurturer, and guide: the role of the teacher. In: Edwards C, Gandini L, Forman, G, eds, *The Hundred Languages of Children*. 2nd edn. USA, Ablex Publishing

Featherstone S, Featherstone P, eds (2008) *Like Bees, not Butterflies: Child-initiated Learning in the Early Years*. London, A&C Black

Gandini L (1998) Educational and caring spaces. In: Edwards C, Gandini L, Forman, G, eds, *The Hundred Languages of Children*. 2nd edn. USA, Ablex Publishing

Glazzard J, Chadwick D, Webster A, Percival J (2010) *Assessment for Learning in the Early Years Foundation Stage*. London, Sage

Helm JH and Katz L (2001) *Young Investigators: The Project Approach in the Early Years*. New York, Teachers College Press

Holt N (2007) *Bringing the High/Scope Approach to your Early Years Practice*. Oxon, Routledge

Howe A, Davies D (2005) Science and play. In: Moyles J, ed, *The Excellence of Play*. 2nd edn. Berkshire, OUP

Hurst V (1994) The implications of the National Curriculum for nursery education. In: Blenkin GM, Kelly AV, eds, *The National Curriculum and Early Learning: An Evaluation*. London, Paul Chapman Publishing

References

Isaacs B (2007) *Bringing the Montessori Approach to Your Early Years Practice*. Oxon, Routledge

Isaacs S (1930) *Intellectual Growth in Young Children*. London, Routledge

Katz LG, Chard SC (1989) *Engaging Children's Minds: The Project Approach*. USA, Ablex Publishing

Katz LG, Chard SC (2000) *Engaging Children's Minds: The Project Approach*. 2nd edn. USA, Ablex Publishing

Lindon J (2008) Child-initiated learning: what does it mean, where does it fit and why is it important for young children? In: Featherstone S, Featherstone P, eds, *Like Bees, not Butterflies: Child-initiated Learning in the Early Years*. London, A&C Black

Mooney CG (2000) *An Introduction to Dewey, Montessori, Erikson, Piaget and Vygotsky*. USA, Redleaf Press

Moyles J (2008) Empowering children and adults: play and child-initiated learning. In: Featherstone S, Featherstone P, eds, *Like Bees, not Butterflies: Child-initiated Learning in the Early Years*. London, A&C Black

Nicol J (2007) *Bringing the Steiner Waldorf Approach to Your Early Years Practice*. Oxon, Routledge

Nutbrown C (2006) *Threads of Thinking*. 3rd edn. London, Sage

Pascal C, Bertram AD, eds (1997) *Effective Early Learning: Case Studies of Improvement*. London, Hodder and Stoughton

Pound L (2006) *How Children Learn*. London, Practical Pre-School Books

Pound L (2009) *How Children Learn 3: Contemporary thinking and theorists*. London, Practical Pre-School Books

Rinaldi C (1998) Projected curriculum constructed through documentation – Progettazione. In: Edwards C, Gandini L, Forman, G, eds, *The Hundred Languages of Children*. 2nd edn. USA, Ablex Publishing

Rinaldi C (2000) The construction of the educational project. In: Rinaldi C (2006) *In Dialogue with Reggio Emilia: Listening, researching and learning*. Oxon, Routledge

Rinaldi C (2001) Teachers as researchers. In: Rinaldi C (2006) *In Dialogue with Reggio Emilia: Listening, researching and learning*. Oxon, Routledge

Scott W (2008) Child-initiated writing. In: Featherstone S, Featherstone P eds, *Like Bees, not Butterflies: Child-initiated Learning in the Early Years*. London, A&C Black

Siraj-Blatchford I (2010) A focus on pedagogy: case studies of effective practice. In: Sylva K, Melhuish E, Sammons P, Siraj-Blatchford I, Taggart B, eds, *Early Childhood Matters: Evidence from the Effective Pre-school and Primary Education Project*. Oxon, Routledge

Thornton L, Brunton P (2007) *Bringing the Reggio Approach to Your Early Years Setting*. Oxon, Routledge

Thornton L, Brunton P (2009) *Understanding the Reggio Approach*. 2nd edn. Oxon, Routledge

Tims C, ed (2010) *Born Creative*. London, Demos. Available from: http://www.demos.co.uk/publications/born-creative-

Vygotsky LS (1978) *Mind in Society*. London, Harvard University Press

Wood E, Attfield J (2005) *Play, Learning and the Early Childhood Curriculum*. London, Paul Chapman Publishing

Government Publications

Bercow J (2008) *The Bercow Report: A Review of Services for Children and Young People (0-19) with Speech, Language and Communication Needs*. Nottingham, DCSF Publications

Central Advisory Council for England (CACE) (1967) *Children and Their Primary Schools* (Plowden Report). London, HMSO. Available from: http://www.educationengland.org.uk/documents/plowden/

Council for the Curriculum Examinations and Assessment (CCEA) (2006) *Northern Ireland Curriculum: Understanding the Foundation Stage*. Belfast, CCEA

Council for the Curriculum Examinations and Assessment (CCEA) (2007) *Northern Ireland Curriculum: Primary*. Belfast, CCEA

Department for Children, Education, Lifelong Learning and Skills (DCELLS) (2008a) *Foundation Phase Framework for Children's Learning for 3 to 7-year-olds in Wales*. Cardiff, DCELLS Publications

Department for Children, Education, Lifelong Learning and Skills (DCELLS) (2008b) *Foundation Phase Framework: Learning and Teaching Pedagogy*. Cardiff, DCELLS Publications

Department for Children, Schools and Families (DCSF) (2007) *The Early Years Foundation Stage: Principles into Practice Cards*. Nottingham, DCSF Publications

Department for Children, Schools and Families (DCSF) (2008) *Statutory Framework for the Early Years Foundation Stage*. (Revised edition) Nottingham, DCSF Publications

Department for Children, Schools and Families (DCSF) (2009) *Learning, Playing and Interacting: Good practice in the Early Years Foundation Stage*. Nottingham, DCSF Publications

Department for Education and Skills (DfES) (2003) *Excellence and Enjoyment*. London, HMSO

Department for Education and Skills (DfES) (2005) *Key Elements of Effective Practice*. Nottingham, DfES Publications

National Assembly for Wales (2003) *The Learning Country: The Foundation Phase – 3 to 7 years*. Consultation document. Cardiff, National Assembly for Wales

New Zealand Ministry of Education (1996) *Te Whāriki: Early Childhood Curriculum*. Wellington, New Zealand, Learning Media Limited

Scottish Executive (2007) *Curriculum for Excellence – Building the curriculum 2: active learning in the early years*. Edinburgh, The Scottish Government

Scottish Government (2008) *Curriculum for Excellence – Building the curriculum 3: a framework for teaching and learning*. Edinburgh, The Scottish Government

Scottish Government (2010) *Curriculum for Excellence – Building the curriculum 5: a framework for assessment: recognising achievement, profiling and reporting*. Edinburgh, The Scottish Government

Swedish Ministry of Education and Science (1998) *Curriculum for the pre-school (Lpfö 98)*. Stockholm, Swedish National Agency for Education

Tickell C (2011) *The Tickell Review: The Early Years: Foundations for life, health and learning*. London, HMSO. Available from: http://www.education.gov.uk/tickellreview

Journals

Gilman S (2007) Including the child with special needs: Learning from Reggio Emilia. *Theory into Practice* 46(1): 23-31

Hewett, L (2001) Examining the Reggio Emilia Approach to early childhood education. *Early Childhood Education Journal* 29(2): 95-100

Laevers F (1993) Deep level learning: an exemplary application on the area of physical knowledge. *European Early Childhood Education Research Journal* 1(1): 53-68

Maslow AH (1943) A theory of human motivation. *Psychological Review* 50(4): 370-396

Maynard T and Chicken S (2010) Through a different lens: exploring Reggio Emilia in a Welsh context. *Early Years* 30(1): 29-39

Siraj-Blatchford I and Sylva K (2004) Researching pedagogy in English pre-schools. *British Educational Research Journal* 30(5): 713-730

Wood D, Bruner J, Ross G (1976) The role of tutoring in problem solving. *Journal of Child Psychology and Psychiatry* 17(2): 89-100

Lectures

Alexander R (2010) Legacies, policies and prospects: One year on from the Cambridge Primary Review. *The 2010 Brian Simon Memorial Lecture*. 6th November 2010. Institute of Education, University of London

References

Professional Articles

Bayley R (2007) Thank you, Mrs Lucas. *Early Years Educator*. 9(4): 14-16

Bloomer K, Cohen B (2008) Children in charge. *Nursery World*. 11th September: 16-17

Brunton P, Thornton L (2005) Let's start viewing young children as researchers. *Early Years Educator*. 6(10): 20-22

Defries M (2008) EYFS protests fail to bring change. *Nursery World*. 29th May: 4

Dowling M (2008) Big ideas. *Nursery World*. 22nd May: 14-16

Gordon-Smith P (2011) All about listening to children. *Nursery World*. 3rd February: 15-19

Howard J, McInnes K (2010) On cue. *Nursery World*. 2nd September: 14-15

Jenkinson Evans S (2010) Documenting creativity. *Early Years Educator*. 12(2): xiv-xvi

O'Connor A (2008) The right stuff. *Nursery World*. 18th December: 14-15

Palmer S (2005) Reclaim Reception! *Child Education*. October: 26-27

Rattigan M (2008) Imagine the difference. *Early Years Educator*. 9(9): viii-ix

Stead K (2009) Project: All together now. *Early Years Educator*. 11(1): Anniversary Supplement 42-46

Thornton L, Brunton P (2004) Curiouser and curiouser. *Nursery World*. 8th January. Available from: www.nurseryworld.co.uk

Research Reports

Moyles J, Adams S, Musgrove A (2002) *Study of Pedagogical Effectiveness in Early Learning*. Research Report No RR363. London, DfES Publications

Organisation for Economic Co-operation and Development (OECD) (2004) *Starting Strong: Curricular and Pedagogies in Early Childhood Education and Care*. Five Curriculum Outlines. Paris, OECD

Siraj-Blatchford I, Sylva K, Muttock S, Gilden R, Bell D (2002a) *Researching Effective Pedagogy in the Early Years [REPEY]*. Research Brief No 356. London, Institute of London, Univeristy of London and Department for Educational Studies, University of Oxford

Siraj-Blatchford I, Sylva K, Muttock S, Gilden R, Bell D (2002b) *Researching Effective Pedagogy in the Early Years [REPEY]*. Research Report No 356. London, HMSO

Siraj-Blatchford I, Sylva K, Melhuish E, Sammons P, Taggart B (2004) *Effective Provision of Pre-school Education [EPPE] Project: Final Report*. London, DfES and Institute of Education, University of London

Training and Support Materials

Bayley R (2006) *Sustained Shared Thinking*. Training delivered in association with States of Jersey Education. October 2006, Jersey, Channel Islands

Dowling M (2005) *Supporting Young Children's Sustained Shared Thinking: An Exploration*. London, The British Association for Early Childhood Education

Young Children's Voices Network (2010) *Let's Listen: Young children's voices – profiling and planning to enable their participation in children's services*. London, National Children's Bureau. Available from: http://www.participationworks.org.uk/files/webfm/files/rooms/early_years/Let'slisten.pdf

Websites

Early Childhood Today (ECT) (2002) ECT Interviews: Lilian G Katz PhD On How Children Learn Through Cooperation. *Early Childhood Today*. Available from: http://www2.scholastic.com/browse/search?query=lilian%20katz

Learning and Teaching Scotland (LTS) (2010) The purpose of the curriculum. *Learning and Teaching Scotland*. Glasgow, Scotland. Available from: http://

www.ltscotland.org.uk/understandingthecurriculum/
whatiscurriculumforexcellence/
thepurposeofthecurriculum/index.asp

Open EYE (2010) *Open EYE: The Campaign for an
Open Early Years Education*. UK, Open EYE. Available
from: www.openeyecampaign.wordpress.com

Index

A

academic subject teaching   15, 17-22, 38
accountability   14-15, 17, 47, 67
active learning   20, 26-31, 35-36
adult-initiated   15, 23-26, 49, 52
adult-led   15, 25-27, 46-47, 51, 53, 60, 63
adult-supported   47, 50, 54, 63
alien provocation   7-8
assessment   6, 15, 41, 51, 54, 57-58, 62, 67
assessment for learning   3

B

Bruce, Tina   12
Bruner, Jerome   29, 34

C

Chard, Sylvia   5-6, 15-17, 20, 28-30, 33, 36, 41, 67
child-centred   3, 9-22, 40-45
child-initiated   11-15, 25-27, 46, 49, 52, 60
cocoon provocation   6, 9-22, 27, 28, 42, 58, 60, 64
cognitive construction   28-29, 35
communicating the project approach   69-71
communication   8, 18-19, 31-36, 37, 40, 47
complexity of project   6, 51
concerns, of practitioners   14-16, 43, 47, 51, 62
concluding a project   65-68
constructivist view   28-29
creativity   16, 18, 28, 36, 38-40
Curriculum for Excellence, Scotland
    4, 9-10, 28, 31, 36, 57
curriculum constraints   4, 6, 10-17, 38, 45-51
Csikszentmihayli, Mihaly   12-13, 16
cycle, planning process   41-58

D

democracy   9-11
developmentally appropriate practice
    10-11, 15-19, 22-31, 34-36
dinosaur land project   6-7
display   58, 64-68
disposition to learn   16-22, 28
documentation   4, 5-6, 15, 41, 53-68
Donaldson, Margaret   17
Dowling, Marion   11, 35-36, 40

E

Early Years Foundation Stage, England
    3, 9, 11, 14-15, 16, 17, 19, 21, 31, 36, 49-51
Effective Early Learning (EEL)   12

Effective Provision for Preschool Education (EPPE)
    23, 35
emotional literacy   18-21
end product   15
English as an additional language
    8, 32-33, 37-39, 42, 45
evidence of learning   15, 67
Excellence and Enjoyment   24
external commitments   16

F

first-hand experience   12, 27-31
flow   12-14
formative assessment   4, 6, 45-51, 58
Foundation Phase Framework, Wales
    10, 11, 16, 19, 31, 36, 57
freedom to explore   12-14
friendship   36
Froboel, Frederick   4, 12, 16, 27
frozen balloons provocation   6, 22-31

G

H

High/Scope   27-28

I

image of the child   9-11
inappropriate tasks   16-18
inclusion   21-22
integrated curriculum   3-4, 14-15
interest of the child
    3, 5-6, 11-14, 16, 21-22, 23-27, 34-35, 40, 41-56, 63
interpretation of documentation   41, 58
involvement   11-14, 20-21
Isaacs, Susan   4, 27

J

joint involvement episodes   34

K

Katz, Lilian
    5-6, 15-17, 19, 20-21, 28-30, 33, 36, 41, 59, 65, 67
Key Elements of Effective Practice (KEEP)   13, 36
knowledge   3-6, 22-25, 28-35, 47, 65-67

L

Laevers, Ferre   12
learning environment
    2-13, 15, 21-24, 27-30, 40, 49, 51-52, 58, 62-65

learning goals   16-17, 20
learning story   4, 28, 31, 66-69
learning styles   23-24, 53
life-long learning   3, 16, 36, 40
listening   11-12, 40, 51, 53-54
literacy   3, 15, 17-20, 28

M
Maslow, Abraham   17
meaningful context for learning
                       3-4, 19-22, 27-28, 32-33
metacommunication   32
Montessori, Maria   12, 16, 27, 28
motivation   9, 12-14, 16-20, 23, 24-25, 31, 44

N
Northern Ireland Curriculum   10, 31, 36
numeracy   17-19, 47
National Curriculum   17, 38
Nutbrown, Cathy   11

O
observation   4, 6, 11-12, 35-36, 41-47, 53-68

P
parents   6, 57, 62, 66-67
pedagogy   9, 23-24, 35-36
performance goals   16-20
personal, social and emotional development   9, 18-21
Pestalozzi, Johann   27
Piaget, Jean   28-29
pirate ship project   6-7
planning   3-6, 11-12, 15, 41, 42-51, 57-65
play   12-15, 18-31, 34, 37
Plowden Report   4, 23
practical experience   12, 20, 26-31, 35-36
Primary Strategies   3, 38
project   4-9
provocation   4-9

Q
questioning   35, 37-39, 40, 47, 54, 58, 62-65

R
rationale   69
Reggio Emilia Approach
              5-6, 11, 21, 28, 32, 34, 41, 47, 49, 53
Researching Effective Pedagogy in the Early Years
(REPEY)   23, 26, 35
Rinaldi, Carla   9, 34-35, 41
routines   7, 14-16, 46

S
scaffolding   28-29, 34-35, 38
schema   11

self-esteem   16-17
Siraj-Blatchford, Iram   26
skills   3-5, 17-22, 29-31, 32-33, 35-40, 59, 62
social constructivist view   33-36
space   9, 12-15, 26, 59, 63
special educational needs   21-22
Steiner, Rudolf   12, 16, 27, 28
Study of Pedagogical Effectiveness in Early Learning
(SPEEL)   23
sustained shared thinking   31, 35-40, 62-68
Swedish Curriculum for the Preschool   18-19

T
Te Whāriki, New Zealand   17-20
Tickell Review   17, 19
themes   3, 29
thinking skills   3, 31-32, 35-40, 59, 62
time   4-6, 12-16, 23, 47, 53, 59, 62, 63, 65
timetable   6-7, 13-14, 16, 62
topics   3-5, 10, 11, 13, 20, 29, 32, 41-42, 49

U
understanding   3-4, 23-35, 44, 46-47, 58, 60, 65, 67

V
Vygotsky, Lev   16, 33-34

W
where is George? provocation   6, 31-40
work   23-24

X

Y

Z
zone of proximal development   34

Acknowledgements

This is the biggest project that I have ever undertaken and I would never have been able to do it without the love and support of my fantastic husband Ged and my beautiful baby boy Harry.

Special thanks must go to Jennie Matthews, Sarah Cahill, Duncan Jacques and all the support staff at Horton Grange Primary School, Bradford, for allowing me into the nursery to carry out the all about eggs project. Thanks must also go of course to all the children who jumped into the experience with so much enthusiasm.

Thank you also to the staff and children at Rawdon Littlemoor Primary School, Leeds, for allowing me to share the cocoon provocation.